TALK | 1

German

JUDITH MATTHEWS
& JEANNE WOOD

Series Editor: Alwena Lamping

In memory of Jeanne Wood, who died shortly before the publication of this book.

BBC Active, an imprint of Educational Publishers LLP, part of the Pearson Education Group, Edinburgh Gate, Harlow, Essex CM20 2JE, England

First published 1998
Eighth edition 2017
8

© Educational Publishers LLP 2014

ISBN: 978-1-406-67892-5

Editors: Naomi Laredo, Anna Miell
New material: Sue Purcell
Project editor: Emma Brown
Insides design: Nicolle Thomas, Rob Lian
Layout: Pantek Media Ltd. www.pantekmedia.co.uk
Illustrations © Mark Duffin
Cover design: Two Associates
Cover photograph: Richard Boll/GETTYIMAGES
Audio producer: John Green, TEFL tapes
Sound engineer: Tim Woolf
Presenters: Wolf Kahler, Aletta Lohmeyer, Peter Stark, Gertrude Thoma
Studio: Robert Nichols Audio Productions
Music: Peter Hutchings

www.bbcactivelanguages.com

Printed and bound in China (CTPSC/08)

The Publisher's policy is to use paper manufactured from sustainable forests.

Pearson Education is not responsible for the content of third-party websites.

Contents

Introduction

Welcome to the new edition of **Talk German**, the bestselling course from BBC Active which has inspired and helped so many people to learn German from scratch and given them the confidence to have a go.

The key to **Talk German**'s effectiveness is the successful **Talk** method, developed by experienced teachers of languages to adult beginners. Its structured and systematic approach encourages you to make genuine progress and promotes a real sense of achievement. The choice of situations and vocabulary is based on the everyday needs of people travelling to Germany.

Talk German includes a book and 120 minutes of recordings of German native speakers. The book in this new edition has several additional features, inspired by feedback from users and teachers. There's an extended grammar section (pages 118–132), a two-way glossary (pages 133–144), covering around 1,000 words, and the ever-popular **Talk** *Wordpower* (pages 130–131), designed to increase your vocabulary fast.

There are also links to the **Talk German** video clips and activities on the BBC Languages website at www.bbcactivelanguages.com/GermanVideoLinks. These cover the contents of this book at the same level but in an alternative way, providing additional exposure and reinforcing the language against the background of German culture. Free tutors' support and activities are available online at www.bbcactivelanguages.com.

How to make the most of Talk German

1 Read the first page of the unit to focus on what you're aiming to learn and set it in context while gaining some relevant vocabulary.

2 Listen to the key phrases – don't be tempted to read them first. Then listen to them again, this time reading them in your book too. Finally, try reading them out loud before listening one more time.

3 Work your way through the activities which follow the key phrases. These highlight key language elements and are carefully designed to develop your listening skills and your understanding of German. You can check your answers at any time in the *Transcripts and answers* starting on page 99.

Wherever you see this: **1•5**, the phrases or dialogues are recorded on the CD (i.e. CD1, track 5).

4 Read the *Auf Deutsch* explanations of how German works as you come to them – this information is placed just where you need it. And if you'd like to know more, visit the relevant pages in the *Grammar* section, indicated by the following symbol: **G13** . For an even deeper level of knowledge, there's a separate **Talk German Grammar** book.

5 After completing the activities, and before you try the *Put it all together* section, listen to the conversations straight through. The more times you listen, the more familiar German will become and the more comfortable you'll become with it. You might also like to read the dialogues at this stage – preferably out loud.

6 Complete the consolidation activities on the *Put it all together* page and check your answers with the *Transcripts and answers*.

7 Use the German you have learnt – the native speaker presenters on the audio will prompt you and guide you through the *Now you're talking*! page as you practise speaking German.

8 Check your progress. First, test your knowledge with the *Quiz*. Then assess whether you can do everything on the checklist – if in doubt, go back and spend some more time on the relevant section.

9 Read the learning hint at the end of the unit, which provides ideas and suggestions on how to use your study time effectively or how to extend your knowledge. Watch the video clip and follow any links that interest you.

10 Finally, relax and listen to the whole unit, understanding what the people are saying in German and taking part in the conversations.

When you've completed the course, go and use your German and enjoy the sense of achievement. If you want to carry on learning, **Talk German 2** is there waiting for you, as is the **Talk German Grammar**, which is so much more than an ordinary grammar book.

Pronunciation guide

Vowels are usually long
- when doubled or followed by **h**: **Tee, Bahn**
- before a single consonant: **gut, Name, Straße**

They are short
- before two or more consonants: **voll, und, dass**

Here are the German letters and letter combinations that are pronounced differently from English, with approximate English equivalents:

Sound	German example(s)	English equivalent
a (long/short)	**Bahnhof/Kaffee**	*rather/sample* (but shorter)
ä (long/short)	**Käse/Kännchen**	*late/get*
au	**Hausfrau, aus**	*now*
äu	**Fräulein**	*oil*
ch (after **a, au, o, u**)	**Nacht, auch**	*loch*
ch (elsewhere)	**ich, nicht**	*human*
chs	**sechs, nächst**	*expel*
e (long/short)	**Tee/Geld**	*hate/met*
ei	**drei, mein**	*mine*
eu	**neun, Deutsch**	*foil*
g (in **-ig**)	**vierzig**	*human*
i (long/short)	**Ihnen/bitte**	*tree/hit*
ie	**Sie, Bier**	*tree*
ie (at end of word)	**Familie**	*pannier*
j	**ja, Januar**	*yet*
o (long/short)	**ohne/Post**	*oh!/lot*
ö (long/short)	**schön/möchte**	*her/men* (spoken with lips pouted)
sch	**Flasche**	*sheep*
sp (at start of word)	**Sport**	*cashpoint*
ß (**Eszett**)	**Straße, heißen**	*pass*
st (at start of word)	**Straße**	*rushed*
u (long/short)	**gut/und**	*June/pull*
ü (long/short)	**für/fünf**	*me/pin* (spoken with lips pursed)
v	**vier**	*fine*
w	**wo**	*vain*
z	**zehn**	*fits*

Guten Tag!

saying hello and goodbye

introducing yourself and socialising

In Deutschland ... *In Germany ...*

as **in Österreich** *in Austria* and **in der Schweiz** *in Switzerland*, people conduct themselves relatively formally and this is evident in the variety of greetings used for different times of day and in different regions of the country. Times are changing, however, and younger generations are less likely to stand on ceremony.

People are also pretty strict on the use of titles. When talking to someone you don't know very well, always use their title and surname, e.g. **Herr** *Mr*, **Frau** *Mrs*, **Dr Pfeiffer**. If in doubt, it's wise to opt for a more formal form of address and then take your lead from the person you're speaking to.

Saying hello

1 **1•02** Listen to these key phrases.

Guten Morgen.	Good morning.
Guten Tag.	Good day./Good afternoon.
Guten Abend.	Good evening.

In all of the above, **guten** can be dropped for informal greetings:

Morgen.   **Tag.**   **Abend.**

2 **1•03** Listen to the members of staff greeting each other as they arrive for work at the Restaurant Franzl. Tick what time of day each of them arrives.

	Morning	Afternoon	Evening
a			
b			
c			
d			
e			

3 **1•03** You may have noticed that some people use first names and some use the title **Herr** (for a man) or **Frau** (for a woman). Listen to the last conversations again and note down how often each is used.

First name ....   **Herr** ....   **Frau** ....

4 **1•04** Listen to these key phrases.

Wie geht es Ihnen?	How are you?
Gut, danke, und Ihnen?	Fine, thank you, and you?

5 **1•05** When people know each other well, they often say **Wie geht's?** Listen to the staff greeting each other at various times of day. How many of these people know each other well?

... and goodbye

6   **1•06** Listen to these key phrases.

Auf Wiedersehen.	Goodbye.
Wiedersehen.	Bye.
Tschüs.	Bye.
Gute Nacht.	Goodnight./Goodbye.

7   **1•07** Four diners are leaving the restaurant and saying goodbye to each other and the staff. Listen and number the speech bubbles below as you hear them.

8   **1•08** Angelika is a receptionist at a large hotel. She speaks to five guests passing through the foyer. How many of them are leaving?

9   How would you greet these people at the times indicated?

11.30 a.m.	Barbara, a good friend
6.15 p.m.	Herr Scholz, restaurant manager
9.00 a.m.	Angelika Hoffmann, hotel receptionist
4.30 p.m.	Manfred, another good friend
7.30 p.m.	Rudi, a waiter

How would you ask Barbara how she is? And how about Herr Scholz?

How would you say goodbye to Manfred? And Rudi?

Introducing yourself

1   1•09 Listen to these key phrases.

Ich heiße ...	I'm called ...
Mein Name ist ...	My name is ...
Wie heißen Sie, bitte?	What's your name/What are you called, please?

2   1•10 At the restaurant, four people who have reserved tables give their names to Ulla, the receptionist. Number them 1 to 4 as you hear them and note down the time of day. You will notice that **Frau** is used as a courtesy title, whatever the age or marital status of the woman.

....	**Anna Blum**	....
....	**Heinrich Müller**	....
....	**Herr Brammerts**	....
....	**Barbara Goldmann**	....

3   1•11 One person walks past without speaking to Ulla, who asks politely who he is. Listen and make a note of the phrase he uses to give his name.

Ulla	**Guten Tag. Wie heißen Sie, bitte?**
Herr Altmann	.... **Altmann, Georg Altmann.**

4   Practise giving your own name, using the same phrase.

Auf Deutsch ... *In German ...*

  bitte is used to oil the wheels of polite conversation. It can mean *please*, as in activity 3 above, but also, among other things, *you're welcome*, *don't mention it* or *here you are*.

... and socialising

5   **1•12** Listen to these key phrases.

Es freut mich./Freut mich.	Pleased to meet you.
Wie bitte?	Pardon?
Und Sie?	And you?

6   **1•13** Georg Altmann and Maria Schwarz meet for the first time. Listen to their conversation and fill the gaps below.

Maria	**Wie heißen ....?**
Georg	**Ich .... Georg Altmann. Und Sie?**
Maria	**Mein .... ist Schwarz, Maria Schwarz.**
Georg	**Wie bitte?**
Maria	**Maria Schwarz.**
Georg	**...................................., Frau Schwarz.**

7   **1•14** Sometimes it's difficult to know if a name is a man's or a woman's. Here are some typical German names, several of which you have already heard. Listen to them and repeat. Check with the pronunciation guide on page 6 if you like.

Women:	**Ulla, Jutta, Inge, Kerstin, Liesl, Ulrike**
Men:	**Dieter, Rudi, Georg, Manfred, Hans, Udo**

8   **1•15** Now listen to four conversations and tick the names that you hear.

Ulla		**Dieter**	
Jutta		**Rudi**	
Inge		**Georg**	
Kerstin		**Manfred**	
Liesl		**Hans**	
Ulrike		**Udo**	

put it **all together**

1   Match the German phrases with their English equivalents.

a	**Auf Wiedersehen.**	How are you?
b	**Wie heißen Sie?**	Pardon?
c	**Tschüs.**	Goodbye.
d	**Guten Tag.**	Pleased to meet you.
e	**Wie bitte?**	What's your name?
f	**Gute Nacht.**	Bye.
g	**Freut mich.**	Goodnight.
h	**Wie geht's?**	Good afternoon.

2   What could these people be saying to each other?

3   Put these sentences into the correct order to make a
    conversation between two people meeting for the first time.

a   **Mein Name ist Blum, Manfred Blum.**
b   **Guten Abend. Wie heißen Sie, bitte?**
c   **Guten Abend.**
d   **Freut mich, Herr Blum.**
e   **Ich heiße Ulrike Müller. Und Sie?**

now you're talking!

Imagine that you're having a drink in the hotel bar before lunch.

1 **1•16** There's a man standing at the bar.

- ◆ Greet him.
- ● **Guten Tag. Wie geht es Ihnen?**
- ◆ Say you're fine and ask how he is.
- ● **Gut, danke.**

2 **1•17** A woman comes in and joins you.

- ◆ Greet her and introduce yourself.
- ● **Freut mich. Ich heiße Schneider, Anna Schneider.**
- ◆ You didn't catch her name. Say *pardon?*
- ● **Frau Schneider, Anna Schneider.**
- ◆ Say you're pleased to meet her.

3 **1•18** Someone else arrives.

- ◆ Greet him and ask his name.
- ● **Mein Name ist Offenbach.**
- ◆ Say you're pleased to meet him. Say who you are.

4 **1•19** Your table is ready.

- ◆ Say goodbye to Frau Schneider and Herr Offenbach.

5 **1•20** You've finished your meal.

- ◆ Say goodbye to Ulla Meyer, who is on duty, and wish her goodnight.

quiz

1 When do you use **Tschüs**?
2 How do you reply if someone says **Wie heißen Sie?**
3 What other way of introducing yourself have you learnt?
4 When do you say **Wie bitte?**
5 What is the German for *pleased to meet you*?
6 It's midnight and you're leaving a party. What do you say?
7 How do you ask an acquaintance how they are?
8 The shop assistant says **Guten Morgen**. What time of day is it?

Now check whether you can ...

- greet someone during the morning, afternoon and evening
- say goodbye
- say goodnight
- introduce yourself
- reply when people introduce themselves to you
- ask someone's name
- ask someone how they are
- reply when someone asks how you are
- ask for clarification if you don't catch what someone says

When you practise speaking, try to imitate the people you hear on the audio. Say the words and phrases out loud and repeat the same thing many times. Once you are confident about saying things, try to build up your speed.

Woher kommen Sie?

saying where you're from

... and where your home town is

saying what you do

using the numbers 0 to 10

In Deutschland ...

each **Land** *state* has a strong regional identity; Bavarians, for example, would describe themselves first and foremost as **Bayer**, speaking their own version of German, **Bayerisch**. Austria (**Österreich**) and the German-speaking part of Switzerland (**die Schweiz**) also have their own regional characteristics in language, food and other aspects of daily life. **Servus!** is used as an informal greeting and farewell in Austria and South Germany. It can mean both *Hi!* and *See you!*

Saying where you're from

1   1•21 Listen to these key phrases.

Woher kommen Sie?	Where do you come from?
Ich komme aus England.	I come from England.
Sind Sie Engländer?	Are you English?
Ja, ich bin Engländer.	Yes, I'm English.
Nein, ich bin Waliserin.	No, I'm Welsh.
Kommen Sie aus	Do you come from Scotland
Schottland oder Irland?	or Ireland?

2   1•22 Brigitte, a courier for an international holiday company, is filling in forms with details of her latest group of tourists. Listen to their conversation. How many of the four people are English?

Auf Deutsch ...

when talking about her nationality or job, a woman usually adds **-in** to whatever a man would say:

Engländer	Engländerin
Kanadier	Kanadierin
Österreicher	Österreicherin

There are some minor variations. For instance:

Schotte	Schottin	*Scottish*
Ire	Irin	*Irish*
Deutscher	Deutsche	*German*

---

3   1•23 Listen to eight more people from Brigitte's group and note down how many are men and how many women.

4   1•23 Listen again and see if you can work out what nationality they are. Many of the words sound very similar to English. They include:

Australier(in)   Amerikaner(in)   Italiener(in)   Spanier(in)

... and where your home town is

5   **1•24** Listen to these key phrases.

Wo wohnen Sie?	Where do you live?
Ich wohne in Wien.	I live in Vienna.
Wo ist das?	Where's that?
Das ist in Österreich.	It's in Austria.
Ich wohne in Padua in Italien.	I live in Padua in Italy.

6   **1•25** Listen to four members of Brigitte's group telling her about themselves and complete the grid below.

Name	Town	Country
Peter Davies	Cardiff	Wales
Irene Fischer		
John McPhee		
Maeve Sullivan		

Auf Deutsch ...

verbs have different endings according to which person they are referring to. The **ich** ending is usually **e**, and the **Sie** ending is almost always **en**:

Ich wohn<u>e</u> in London.	Wohn<u>en</u> Sie in Wien?
Ich komm<u>e</u> aus England.	Komm<u>en</u> Sie aus Österreich? **G8**

---

7   **1•26** Listen to these short conversations and fill the gaps.

Georg	**Wo .... Sie, Frau Schwarz?**
Maria	**Ich .... in Wien in Österreich.**
Maria	**................ wohnen Sie?**
Anna	**Ich wohne .... Bozen in ....**
Maria	**Und wo wohnen ....? Sind Sie Italiener?**
Carlos	**Nein, ich bin Spanier. .... wohne in Madrid.**

Saying what you do

1 **1•27** Listen to these key phrases.

Was sind Sie?	What are you?/What do you do?
Ich bin Sekretär(in).	I'm a secretary.
Ich bin Mechaniker(in).	I'm a mechanic.
Ich bin arbeitslos.	I'm unemployed.

Auf Deutsch ...

when giving your nationality or job, *a* is not used:

Ich bin Hausfrau.   *I'm a housewife.*
Ich bin Lehrer(in).   *I'm a teacher.*

Have you noticed that all German nouns are written with a capital letter?

G4

2 Look at these jobs and see if you can identify the German equivalent of *policewoman*, *student* and *computer programmer*.

Sekretär	**Student**
Polizistin	**Hausfrau**
Programmierer	**Lehrerin**

How many of these words do you think refer to women? ....

3 **1•28** Brigitte asks these members of her tour group what their occupations are. Listen and note them down in English.

Maeve Sullivan	....
Irene Fischer	....
Mark Smith	....
Elena Pastena	....
John McPhee	....
Peter Davies	....

Using the numbers 0 to 10

1 **1•29** Look at the following numbers 0 to 10 and then listen to them on the audio.

0	1	2	3	4	5	6	7	8	9	10
null	**eins**	**zwei**	**drei**	**vier**	**fünf**	**sechs**	**sieben**	**acht**	**neun**	**zehn**

2 **1•30** Listen to the numbers being called for a game of **Lotto** *bingo* and circle those which appear on your card below.

1	3	8
2	6	10

Auf Deutsch ...

as you may have noticed, **zwei** and **drei** sound very similar, so to prevent confusion, German speakers often substitute **zwo** for **zwei** when giving important numbers.

3 **1•31** Brigitte asks Irene, Mark and Peter what their telephone number is: **Was ist Ihre Telefonnummer?**
What are their numbers?

Irene .... Mark .... Peter ....

4 **1•32** Practise saying the telephone numbers on the right out loud, then check by listening to the recording.

704568
591674
1253 6732
853197

5 Practise saying your own number, at home and/or at work.

put it all together

1   Match the questions and the answers.

a Sind Sie Amerikaner oder Kanadier?	Ich bin Hausfrau.
b Woher kommen Sie?	01982 46723
c Kommen Sie aus Schottland?	Ich wohne in Stirling.
d Wo wohnen Sie?	Aus Amerika.
e Was sind Sie?	Nein, ich komme aus Irland.
f Was ist Ihre Telefonnummer?	Ich bin Kanadier.

2   Read the descriptions given to Brigitte by three more tourists and complete the grid in English.

a   Ich heiße Helen Brownsmith. Ich bin Amerikanerin. Ich wohne in Washington und ich bin Lehrerin.

b   Ich bin Österreicher. Ich heiße Georg Müller. Ich bin Programmierer und ich wohne in Salzburg.

c   Mein Name ist Andrew Hyde. Ich bin Schotte und ich wohne in Glasgow. Ich bin Polizist.

Name	Nationality	Home town	Job
Helen Brownsmith			
		Salzburg	
	Scottish		

3   Using the descriptions in activity 2 as a guide, work out what Dieter and Juanita would say about themselves.

Dieter Hoffman
Austrian,
from Vienna
unemployed

Juanita Pueblos
Spanish,
from Madrid
student

now you're talking!

1   1•33 When the tour reaches Dresden, the party splits up
    into small groups to visit the town. Helen gets talking to
    a customer in a shop. Answer as if you were Helen, giving
    information about yourself from the grid on the page opposite.
    The customer begins by asking *Are you a foreigner?*

- **Sind Sie Ausländerin?**
- ◆ Say yes and tell her your nationality.
- **Wo wohnen Sie?**
- ◆ Say where you live.
- **Was sind Sie?**
- ◆ Say what you do.

2   1•34 David, another member of the group, has a similar
    conversation in a bar. Answer for him.

> **Name:** David Jones
> **Nationality:** Welsh
> **Home town:** Cardiff
> **Occupation:** Mechanic
> **Phone no:** 01643 9758

- **Herr Jones, sind Sie Engländer?**
- **Wo wohnen Sie in Wales?**
- **Was sind Sie?**
- **Und was ist Ihre Telefonnummer?**

3   1•35 Georg initiates a conversation in a café. Ask the
    questions for him.

- ◆ Ask the person's name.
- **Ich heiße Ulrike Dietrich.**
- ◆ Ask where she lives.
- **Ich wohne in Kiel in Deutschland.**
- ◆ Ask what she does.
- **Ich bin Stewardess bei Lufthansa.**

quiz

1 How does an American woman give her nationality?
2 How would you ask someone if they live in Leipzig?
3 How would you tell someone that you're from Chester?
4 How would you respond to the question **Sind Sie Italiener(in)?**
5 How does a woman student say what she does?
6 If a man says he is **Österreicher**, where is he from?
7 Fill in the missing numbers:
   drei, ..., **fünf**, **sechs**, ..., **acht**
8 Which is the odd one out?
   Lehrer, **Schottin**, **Hausfrau**, **Sekretärin**, **Polizist**

Now check whether you can ...

- say what nationality you are
- say which country you are from
- say which town you live in
- say what work you do
- ask others for this information
- give your telephone number

It's a good idea at this stage to start organising your vocabulary learning. Write new words down in a book, put them on sticky labels in places where you can't fail to notice them, record them and get someone to test you on them. (It need not be a German speaker.) Make your vocabulary list relevant to you and your lifestyle. It's much easier to learn and retain words which are important to you.

Zwei Kaffee, bitte

ordering a drink in a bar

... and in a café

offering someone a drink

... and accepting or refusing

In Deutschland ...

in Österreich und in der Schweiz, as in many other European countries, café life is popular. People relax for long periods over a cup of coffee; local and national newspapers are often available for customers to read. For people in a hurry, there is also the **Stehcafé** – literally, *standing café* – where you can buy tea or coffee and perhaps a cake at the counter and stand to consume it at the nearest table. There are many varieties of coffee; the choice depends on the region. Most come with milk or cream, so you have to say how you want your coffee served.

Ordering a drink in a bar

1   **1•36** Listen to these key phrases.

Bitte schön?	Can I help you?
Ein Bier, bitte.	A beer, please.
Ein Glas Rotwein.	A glass of red wine.
Ein Glas Weißwein.	A glass of white wine.
Ein Mineralwasser.	A mineral water.
Ich möchte eine Cola.	I'd like a cola.

2   **1•37** Listen to people ordering these drinks and number them as you hear them.

....   **ein Mineralwasser**

....   **ein Glas Rotwein**

....   **eine Cola**

....   **ein Bier**

3   **1•38** Some of the tourists in Brigitte's group go into a bar. Listen to Helen, Georg, Irene and Peter and note down in English what they order.

Helen ....

Georg ....

Irene ....

Peter ....

... and in a café

4 1•39 Listen to these key phrases.

Eine Tasse Kaffee, bitte.	A cup of coffee, please.
Ein Kännchen Tee.	A pot of tea.
Eine Schokolade.	A drinking chocolate.
mit Sahne	with cream
ohne Milch	without milk
Zwei Tassen Tee.	Two cups of tea.
Sonst noch etwas?	Anything else?

5 1•40 Now listen to six people ordering drinks and tick the boxes to show what they want.

	a	b	c	d	e	f
ein Kännchen Tee						
eine Tasse Tee						
ein Kännchen Kaffee						
eine Tasse Kaffee						
mit Milch						
ohne Milch						
mit Sahne						
eine Schokolade						

Auf Deutsch ...

when ordering drinks, most words don't change in the plural: **ein Bier, zwei Bier; ein Glas Rotwein, drei Glas Rotwein**. One that does change is **Tasse: eine Tasse Tee, zwei Tassen Tee**. German plurals are formed in a variety of ways, so it is best to learn the ones you need as you meet them.   **G3**

---

6 How would you ask for the following?

- a pot of tea with milk
- a cup of tea without milk
- a pot of coffee
- two cups of coffee with cream

Offering someone a drink

1   **1●41** Listen to these key phrases.

Was möchten Sie?	What would you like?
Möchten Sie einen Kaffee?	Would you like a coffee?
Und für Sie?	And for you?
Noch einen Kaffee?	Another coffee?

2   **1●42** Listen to the conversation and fill the gaps below.

Georg   **Maria, was .... Sie?**
Maria   **Oh, ein .... Wein, bitte.**
Georg   **Ein Glas ....?**
Maria   **Nein, ...**
Georg   **Und .... Sie, Franz? .... einen Kaffee?**

Auf Deutsch ...

nouns divide into three categories or 'genders' – masculine, feminine and neuter – and this affects words used with them, like *a* and *the*. They're also affected by the way the noun is used in the sentence. When you ask for or offer something, the word for *a* is as follows:

möchten Sie <u>einen</u> Kaffee? – masculine (m)

möchten Sie <u>eine</u> Tasse Tee? – feminine (f)

möchten Sie <u>ein</u> Bier? – neuter (n)   G2, G4

---

3   How would you offer someone these drinks?

- a coffee
- a glass of beer
- a cup of tea with milk
- another coffee
- a coke

... and accepting or refusing

4 1•43 Listen to these key phrases.

Gern.	I'd love one.
Ja, danke.	Yes, thank you.
Danke schön.	Thank you very much.
Nichts für mich, danke.	Nothing for me, thank you.
Nein, danke.	No, thank you.
Prost!	Cheers!

5 1•44 Georg offers several people drinks. Listen and tick the ones who accept.

Barbara

Irene

Franz

Manfred

Angelika

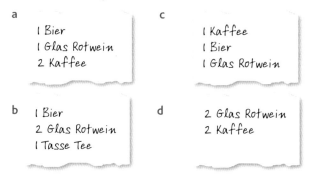

Prost!

6 1•44 Listen to the conversation in activity 5 again and decide which of the bills is Georg's.

a
1 Bier
1 Glas Rotwein
2 Kaffee

b
1 Bier
2 Glas Rotwein
1 Tasse Tee

c
1 Kaffee
1 Bier
1 Glas Rotwein

d
2 Glas Rotwein
2 Kaffee

7 And now decide what to say when ...

- you raise your glass to your friends
- you thank someone very much for their offer

put it all together

1 Irene is at the bar, ordering three glasses of white wine and a beer. The man next to her is ordering three beers, a coke and a mineral water. Make a note of what each will say in German.

Irene ....

Mann ....

2 Which is the right phrase for each situation?

   1 You refuse the offer of a coffee.
      a **Prost!**   b **Nein, danke.**
      c **Ohne Sahne.**

   2 You offer someone a drink.
      a **Bitte schön?**   b **Sonst noch etwas?**
      c **Was möchten Sie?**

   3 You would like your coffee with milk.
      a **Mit Milch.**   b **Ohne Milch.**
      c **Mit Sahne.**

   4 You'd love to accept a glass of red wine.
      a **Und für Sie?**   b **Für mich nichts.**
      c **Gern.**

3 Complete this conversation with the waiter (**Ober**) in a restaurant, using the words in the box.

Ober	**Guten Abend. Bitte schön?**
Jutta	**Ich .... Kaffee, bitte.**
	Und für ...., Liesl?
Liesl	**Für .... ein Bier.**
Jutta	**Und Sie, Manfred?**
Manfred	**Für mich ...., ...**
Jutta	**Gut. Ein Bier und einen Kaffee, ...**
Ober	**Sonst noch etwas?**
Jutta	**................, danke.**

möchte
nein
mich
bitte
Sie
danke
nichts
einen

now you're **talking!**

1   **1•45** You meet two colleagues in a café. One of them offers you a drink.

- ● **Möchten Sie einen Kaffee?**
- ◆ Say yes, you'd love one.
- ● **Mit oder ohne Sahne?**
- ◆ Say *With cream, please*.

  Now it's your turn to order.
- ◆ Ask Franz what he would like.
- ● **Ein Mineralwasser, bitte.**
- ◆ Ask Irene if she'd like another coffee.
- ● **Ja, danke.**
- ◆ Order a mineral water, a cup of coffee and a pot of tea.

2   **1•46** You are out with a large group of friends and have noted down what they want to drink. The waitress comes over.

- ● **Bitte schön.**
- ◆ Ask for a cup of tea with milk and two pots of coffee.

  Later, a waiter comes up to you.
- ● **Bitte schön.**
- ◆ Order a glass of white wine, two glasses of coke and four beers.

3   **1•47** Now take part in a conversation in a bar. The waiter approaches.

- ● **Bitte schön?**
- ◆ Ask your companion if she would like a beer.
- ● **Ja, gern.**
- ◆ You are joined by Dieter and Kerstin. Offer Dieter a drink.
- ● **Für mich ein Glas Bier.**
- ◆ And Kerstin?
- ● **Für mich ein Glas Rotwein.**
- ◆ Give the waiter the order, plus a glass of white wine for you.
- ● **Sonst noch etwas?**
- ◆ Say no thank you.
- ◆ The drinks arrive. Thank the waiter, then say *Cheers!*

quiz

1 If you order **Kaffee mit Milch**, will it be white or black?

2 **Rotwein, Weißwein** – which is the red wine?

3 You offer someone a drink and they say **gern**. Are they accepting or refusing?

4 **Noch drei Bier** – what have you ordered?

5 What does the waiter want to know if he says **Sonst noch etwas?**

6 Name two alcoholic drinks in German.

7 Which of these drinks could you have **mit Sahne**?

   Cola, Kaffee, Tee

8 You want a pot of tea. Do you ask for **eine Tasse** or **ein Kännchen**?

Now check whether you can ...

- order a drink
- offer someone a drink
- accept when someone offers you a drink
  ... or refuse politely
- say how you want your drink
- order more drinks
- say *Cheers!*

When you meet a word for the first time, it's a good idea to check in the glossary whether it's masculine, feminine or neuter. Nouns are listed there with the word for *the*, which shows which category they belong to: **der Kaffee** (m), **die Schokolade** (f), **das Bier** (n). You'll find it quite easy to remember if you learn each word together with **der**, **die** or **das** as you go along.

Darf ich vorstellen?

introducing someone

talking about family

asking and giving someone's age

using the numbers up to 100

In Deutschland ...

in Österreich und in der Schweiz, families still gather at traditional times, especially to celebrate Christmas and New Year. Many regions have their own distinctive ways of celebrating these and other festivals, and the predominantly Catholic southern areas have extra public holidays associated with saints' days. Despite changing work patterns, many people stay in their home region and thus maintain close family ties.

Introducing someone

1 1•48 Listen to these key phrases.

Darf ich vorstellen?	May I introduce (to you)?
Das ist mein Mann.	This is my husband.
Das ist meine Frau.	This is my wife.
Das sind meine Freunde.	These are my friends.
Freut mich.	Pleased to meet you.
Ebenfalls.	Likewise. (Pleased to meet you too.)

Auf Deutsch ...

Frau and Herr, as you will remember, mean *Mrs* and *Mr*. **Frau** has additional meanings: **meine Frau** means *my wife* and **eine Frau** means *a woman*. The word for *man* and *husband*, however, is **Mann**, not Herr.

Notice that *my* has different forms depending on the noun it's used with: **mein Mann** (m), but **meine Frau** (f).

G9

2 1•49 Some members of the tour group are getting to know each other. Listen and fill the gaps in their conversations.

a *Irene Fischer*   **Darf ich** ....**? Das** .... **mein Mann, Karl Fischer.**

   Joachim Schneider   **Freut mich. Mein Name ist Joachim Schneider.**

b *Joachim Schneider*   .... **ich vorstellen? Das** .... **meine Freunde, Bob und Joan Butler.**

   Irene Fischer   **Es freut mich, Herr Butler, Frau Butler.**

   Bob Butler   ....

3 Liesl and Hans are a married couple. How would each introduce the other?

   Liesl   **Darf ich vorstellen?** ....

   Hans   ....

Talking about family

1   1•50 Listen to these key phrases.

Sind Sie verheiratet?	Are you married?
Ja, ich bin verheiratet.	Yes, I'm married.
Nein, ich bin nicht verheiratet.	No, I'm not married.

2   1•51 Listen to Joachim Förster talking to Brigitte and her colleagues, Herr Koch and Frau Schwarz. Who is married?

3   1•52 Listen to these key phrases.

Haben Sie Kinder?	Have you any children?
Ich habe keine Kinder.	I don't have children.
Ja, ich habe ...	Yes, I have ...
... eine Tochter/zwei Töchter.	... a daughter/two daughters.
... einen Sohn/drei Söhne.	... a son/three sons.

Auf Deutsch ...

like **ein** and **mein**, **kein** *no, not any* varies in form. The masculine forms **ein/mein/kein** change to **einen/meinen/keinen** when used with the object of the sentence (i.e. what you have, want, like, etc.):

Das ist mein Sohn.	**Ich habe einen/keinen Sohn.**
Das ist meine Tochter.	**Ich habe eine/keine Tochter.**

The form with plurals is the same as with feminine nouns:

Das sind meine Töchter.	**Ich habe keine Kinder.** **G2, G4**

---

4   1•53 Listen to Brigitte asking for information and complete the form.

Name:	Familienstand:	Kinder:
Irene Fischer	verheiratet	
Joachim Schneider		
Georg Müller		

Asking and giving someone's age

1   1•54 Listen to these key phrases.

Wie alt sind Sie?	How old are you?
Ich bin vierundzwanzig Jahre alt.	I'm 24 years old.
Wie alt ist er? Er ist fünfzehn.	How old is he? He's 15.
Mein Sohn ist sechzehn.	My son is 16.
Wie alt ist sie? Sie ist elf.	How old is she? She's 11.
Meine Tochter ist zwölf.	My daughter is 12.

2   1•55 Now listen to all the numbers from 11 to 19. You'll recognise 3 to 9 in the numbers 13 to 19.

11 **elf**, 12 **zwölf**, 13 **dreizehn**, 14 **vierzehn**, 15 **fünfzehn**,
16 **sechzehn**, 17 **siebzehn**, 18 **achtzehn**, 19 **neunzehn**

3   1•56 Listen and note down the ages of these children.

Fritz ....   *Maria* ....   *Liesl* ....   *Jutta* ....

4   How would Herr Altmann state his children's ages?

★★★ **Campingplatz am Rheinufer**

Name: Altmann............................

Kinder: Manfred 19; Angelika 16; Daniel 11

Mein Sohn Manfred ....

Meine ....

....

Using the numbers up to 100

1   **1•57** Listen to the numbers 20 to 25.

20 **zwanzig**	23 **dreiundzwanzig**
21 **einundzwanzig**	24 **vierundzwanzig**
22 **zweiundzwanzig**	25 **fünfundzwanzig**

2   **1•58** Before you listen to 26 to 29, try to fill the gaps.

26 ....**undzwanzig**	28 ....**undzwanzig**
27 **siebenund**...........................	29 **neun**...........................

In German, the numbers above 20 are written and spoken in
the reverse order to English: **einundzwanzig** – *one and twenty*,
zweiundzwanzig – *two and twenty*, and so on.

3   **1•59** Now listen to these larger numbers.

30 **dreißig**	60 **sechzig**	90 **neunzig**
40 **vierzig**	70 **siebzig**	100 **hundert**
50 **fünfzig**	80 **achtzig**	

Hundert on its own means *a hundred* or *one hundred*.

4   The pattern you saw in 21 to 29 is repeated in numbers up to 100.
Complete the numbers 41 to 49.

41 **einundvierzig**	44 **vierundvierzig**	47 **sieben**........**vierzig**
42 **zweiundvierzig**	45 ....**undvierzig**	48 **achtundvierzig**
43 ....**undvierzig**	46 **sechsund**........	49 ....

5   **1•60** Listen to people talking about their families and circle the
number you hear in each of these pairs.

a	23	32		d	70	17
b	15	50		e	59	94
c	46	64				

put it all together

1   The Bradshaws are planning a house swap with Familie Friedmann. Read what Dieter writes about his family.

Darf ich vorstellen? Mein Name ist Dieter Friedmann. Ich bin verheiratet und habe einen Sohn und eine Tochter. Ich bin vierundvierzig Jahre alt, meine Frau Kerstin ist achtunddreißig. Mein Sohn Helmut ist fünfzehn und meine Tochter Susanna ist elf.

Write an introduction from Jack about the Bradshaws. Here is the information about them.

Jack aged 48
Mary aged 47
Frank aged 26
Julia aged 24

2   Put these sentences into the correct order to make a conversation between Joachim Schneider and Heinz Wolf.

   a   **Wie alt ist Grete?**
   b   **Ja, meine Frau heißt Julia. Und Sie?**
   c   **Sie ist zwölf.**
   d   **Sind Sie verheiratet, Herr Wolf?**
   e   **Ja, ich habe eine Tochter, Grete.**
   f   **Nein, ich bin nicht verheiratet. Haben Sie Kinder?**

3   Match the family to the house.

Familie Förster zweiundfünfzig	Familie Lindemann neunundvierzig	Familie Martens einundfünfzig	Familie Schröder achtundvierzig

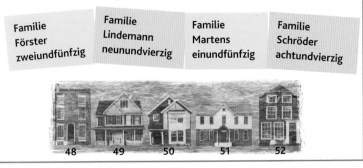

48   49   50   51   52

now you're talking!

Take the part of Robert Blythe, who is talking to a fellow guest in the hotel lounge.

1 **1•61** Your new acquaintance asks about you and your family. Read the questions and prepare your answers before speaking.

Clare   Robert   Jenny, 11

Wie heißen Sie? ....

Sind Sie verheiratet? ....

Und haben Sie Kinder? ....

Haben Sie einen Sohn? ....

Wie alt ist Jenny? ....

2 **1•62** Two more people join you. Your new acquaintance introduces them.

- **Darf ich vorstellen? Das sind meine Freunde, Stephanie und Georg Krumm ... Herr Blythe.**
- **Freut mich, Herr Blythe.**
- ◆ Respond to Frau Krumm's greeting.

Just then, your wife arrives.
- ◆ Introduce her to Mr and Mrs Krumm.
- **Freut mich, Frau Blythe.**

3 **1•63** Ask Mrs Krumm these questions and listen to her replies:

- ◆ Has she any children?
- ◆ How old is her son?

quiz

1 How would a woman introduce her husband?

2 Someone says **Freut mich**. What might you reply?

3 If someone says **Ich habe keine Kinder**, what are they telling you?

4 How do you say how old you are in German?

5 If someone says **Ich bin achtzehn Jahre alt**, are they 8, 18 or 80?

6 When referring to a daughter, would you say **sie** or **er**?

7 Does the word **verheiratet** describe a married or a single person?

8 How does someone say that they have three sons?

Now check whether you can ...

- introduce someone – male or female
- give your age
- say how old someone else is
- ask other people for this information
- say whether you are married
- say whether you have any children
- say how many sons and daughters you have
- use the numbers 11 to 100

At this early stage in your language learning, the secret is to keep it simple. You can pick up the words of a question to form your answer: **Sind Sie verheiratet?** can help you to answer **Ja, ich bin verheiratet**. And **Nein, ich bin nicht verheiratet** will cover separated, divorced and widowed, as well as single. You will be surprised how much you can convey with a few words.

Kontrollpunkt 1

1 Choose the appropriate expression for each situation.

> **Guten Abend!** **Prost!** **Aus England.** **Nein, danke.**
> **Ja, einen Sohn.** **Sind Sie verheiratet?** **Gute Nacht.**

a Answering **Haben Sie Kinder?** ....

b Saying *Cheers!* ....

c Refusing an offer of a drink. ....

d Greeting someone at 7 p.m. ....

e Asking if someone is married. ....

f Saying goodnight/goodbye. ....

g Answering **Woher kommen Sie?** ....

2 **1•64** Listen to Detlev and Sylvia as they get to know each other at a party, and fill in the information you learn in the grid below.

Name	Nationality	Occupation	Family
Detlev			
Sylvia			

3 **1•65** Brigitte has filled in a form for two of her tourists, but she was tired and made a number of errors. Listen and correct the form.

> **Name:** *Miller, Margaret* *Carter, Steven*
>
> **Nationalität:** *Kanadierin* *Engländer*
>
> **Beruf:** *Polizistin* *Lehrer*
>
> **Alter:** *35* *42*
>
> **Familie:** *einen Sohn* *keine Kinder*

4 **1•66** Brigitte and Joachim are joined for a drink by Irene and Georg. Listen and note in English what each one has.

Brigitte .... *Irene* ....

Georg .... *Joachim* ....

5 **1•67**

    a Say the following numbers aloud and then check by listening to the audio.

        71   12   89   45   54

    b Brigitte is giving Martha her phone number. Listen and tick the correct number below.

        178263 ☐   **168263** ☐   **178253** ☐

6   Rudi, the waiter, is applying for a job in England and would like help in filling in his application form. What questions would you need to ask him in order to find out the missing information?

Name:	.... a ....
Address:	Rudolfstraße 14, DRESDEN ....
Tel. no:	065 435 98
Age:	.... b ....
Marital status:	.... c ....
Nationality:	German ....
Occupation:	.... d ....

    a ....

    b ....

    c ....

    d ....

7   **1•68** You're in a café, ordering for yourself and some friends. Barbara wants a cup of coffee; Carla wants a lemonade; Michael wants a beer; Rolf wants a glass of red wine and you want a glass of white wine. What will you say to the waiter when he comes up and asks for your order? Listen to the audio to see if you're right.

8   A neighbour's son receives a letter from a new German penfriend.
    Some words, or parts of words, are unreadable because the letter
    got wet. Help him to reconstruct it and answer his questions below.
    (Check the unfamiliar words in the glossary after you have made a
    guess at what they mean.)

> Stuttgart
> I. August
>
> Lieber Paul,
>
> ich heiße Tobias und wohne in Deutschland,
> in Stuttgart. Ich bin 14 Jahre alt. Mein Vater ist
> Programmierer und meine Mutter ist Sekretärin
> bei Woolworths. Ich habe eine Schwester, Susi, und
> einen Bruder, Jochen. Susi ist 19 und ist Studentin
> an der Universität Marburg. Jochen ist 22 und ist
> schon verheiratet. Seine Frau kommt aus Italien.
> Er ist arbeitslos und sie ist Lehrerin.

Missing words: ....
....
....

a   What do Tobias' brother and sister do?
    ....

b   What do Tobias' father and mother do?
    ....

c   How old is Tobias?
    ....

d   What nationality is Jochen's wife?
    ....

9   Can you find the German words for the following, hidden in the grid?
    They are written upwards or downwards, left to right or right to left.
    (Umlauts have been omitted.)

a   Good morning.   ....
b   Goodbye. (formal)   ....
c   Goodbye. (informal)   ....
d   My name is …   ....
e   Pleased to meet you.   ....
f   Thank you.   ....
g   I am …   ....
h   Good evening.   ....
i   How are you? (formal)   ....

G	U	T	E	N	M	O	R	G	E	N	A
R	A	N	K	S	E	I	T	U	B	E	U
W	L	T	N	C	I	H	E	T	I	N	F
K	N	E	A	H	N	A	D	E	S	H	W
O	I	S	D	A	R	N	E	N	H	I	I
R	K	E	H	L	P	O	K	A	C	S	E
T	W	I	S	T	M	R	A	B	U	E	D
T	R	S	U	H	C	S	T	E	T	T	E
O	H	C	I	R	N	I	G	N	L	H	R
G	C	A	C	H	E	M	E	D	I	E	S
S	S	R	H	A	S	T	D	E	M	G	E
S	U	M	B	S	E	E	G	S	K	E	H
U	H	C	I	M	T	U	E	R	F	I	E
R	B	O	N	F	I	R	U	A	C	W	N
G	T	S	I	E	M	A	N	N	I	E	M

Wo ist die Bank?

enquiring about places in town

... and understanding where they are

following simple directions

asking for help with understanding

In Deutschland ...

in Österreich und in der Schweiz, the market square (**Marktplatz**), with the town hall (**Rathaus**) and often a fountain (**Brunnen**), is still the heart of many small towns. Most modern cities retain their old town centre (**Altstadt**) with its historic buildings. Every town has an information office which you will recognise by the international 'i' symbol for information (**Auskunft**). You will still see tourist offices in some small towns called **Verkehrsamt**, **Verkehrsverein** or **Verkehrsbüro**, but the terms **Touristinfo** and **Touristeninformationen** (sometimes hyphenated **Touristen-Informationen**) are more common these days.

Enquiring about places in town

1 1•69 Listen to these key phrases.

Entschuldigen Sie …	Excuse me …
Wo ist die Bank?	Where's the bank?
Wo ist der Bahnhof?	Where's the station?
Ist das die Post?	Is that the post office?
Ist das weit von hier?	Is it far from here?

2 1•70 Five tourists stop Rudi on the street to ask about these places.
Listen and number them in the order you hear them.

die Post

die Bank

das Rathaus

der Marktplatz

der Bahnhof

Auf Deutsch …

the word for *the* is **der** with a masculine noun (**der Bahnhof**),
die with a feminine noun (**die Post**) and **das** with a neuter one
(**das Rathaus**).   G4

3 1•71 Now listen to more tourists asking about places and fill the
blanks in the sentences below. You will hear the words for *the
cathedral* and *the shopping centre*; you can check in the glossary if you
are not sure which is which.

a **Entschuldigen Sie, ... der Bahnhof, bitte?**
b **Wo ist der Dom? Ist das .... von hier?**
c **Wo ist ...., bitte?**
d **................................ Sie, ist das das Verkehrs ....?**
e **Ist das Einkaufszentrum weit ....?**

... and understanding where they are

4 **1•72** Listen to these key phrases.

Wir sind hier.	We are here.
Die Post ist links.	The post office is on the left.
Die Bank ist rechts.	The bank is on the right.
Da drüben.	Over there.
Geradeaus.	Straight on.
Es ist fünf Minuten zu Fuß.	It's five minutes on foot.

5 **1•73** Brigitte is showing Irene where places are on a plan of Neustadt, including **die Apotheke** *the chemist's*. Listen and note down the places mentioned. Then listen again and mark each place R (right), L (left), S (straight on) or O (over there).

a .... d ....

b .... e ....

c ....

6 Read the information below and label the places numbered 1 to 5 on the map.

Das Verkehrsamt ist links. Die Apotheke ist hier rechts und das Rathaus ist da drüben rechts. Der Dom ist geradeaus am Marktplatz und der Bahnhof ist auch geradeaus – fünf Minuten zu Fuß.

7 How would you ask where these places are?

- the station
- the tourist office
- the cathedral

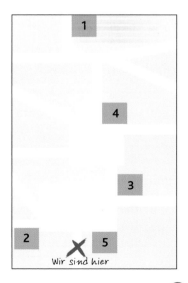

Following simple directions

1 **1•74** Listen to these key phrases.

Gehen Sie ...	Go ...
... um die Ecke.	... round the corner.
... hier links.	... left here.
Nehmen Sie ...	Take ...
... die erste Straße rechts.	... the first road on the right.
... die zweite Straße links.	... the second road on the left.
Das ist neben dem Museum.	It's next to the museum.
gegenüber dem Bahnhof	opposite the station
nicht weit von der Post	not far from the post office

2 **1•75** A Neustadt tourist office employee is answering tourists' questions. As you listen, tick the correct instructions below, then correct the ones that are wrong.

a **Der Dom? Gehen Sie geradeaus und dann rechts.**
b **Das Verkehrsamt ist da drüben, neben der Bank.**
c **Der Bahnhof ist hier links.**
d **Das Einkaufszentrum ist rechts um die Ecke.**
e **Der Dom ist gegenüber der Bank.**
f **Nehmen Sie die zweite Straße rechts und die Apotheke ist neben der Post.**

Auf Deutsch ...

after some locating words, including **gegenüber**, **neben** and **von**:

- **der** and **das** change to **dem**: gegenüber **dem** Bahnhof
- **die** changes to **der**: von **der** Post **G6**

---

3 Complete these directions.

a **Das Museum ist neben .... Bahnhof.**
b **Der Parkplatz ist nicht weit von .... Bank.**
c **Die Post ist gegenüber .... Einkaufszentrum.**
d **Der Dom ist neben .... Marktplatz.**

Asking for help with understanding

1 1•76 Listen to these key phrases.

Bitte wiederholen Sie.   Please repeat that.
Sprechen Sie langsamer, bitte.   Please speak more slowly.
Ich verstehe nicht.   I don't understand.
Ich bin fremd hier.   I'm a stranger here.

Auf Deutsch ...

as in other languages, words are often used which don't add
essential information to the sentence. Listen out in this unit for
dann, vielleicht and **auch**, and see if you can work out what they
mean. The answers are given later.

---

2 1•77 Listen to Rudi helping some tourists on his way to work. Note
down in English the place each one is looking for. Listen a second time
and note (also in English) what problem each one has.

	Place	Problem
Irene		
Anna		
Maria		
Jutta		

3 Which of the phrases above would you use in the following situations?
(There may be more than one possible answer, or you could use a
combination of phrases.)

a You ask someone for information; they think you are a fluent speaker
and reply very quickly.
b You don't know the town and ask a passer-by for help.
c Someone gives you directions, but you can't take it all in at once.
d Someone uses a lot of words which are new to you.

put it all together

1   How would you ask where these places are?

a   b   c

d   e   f

a   ....

b   ....

c   ....

d   ....

e   ....

f   ....

2   Follow the directions below on the map and write down
    where you get to.

   a   **Gehen Sie geradeaus, nehmen Sie die zweite
       Straße links. Das ist da links.**
   b   **Das ist da drüben rechts.**
   c   **Gehen Sie hier rechts um die Ecke.
       Das ist neben der Post.**
   d   **Gehen Sie geradeaus.**

3   Look at the map again and
    write down the directions
    for:

   a   the museum

       ....

   b   the bank

       ....

Marktplatz

Bank

Einkaufszentrum   Museum

                            i

                         Post

Wir sind hier ✗

now you're talking!

1   **1•78** Before leaving your hotel to look round Neustadt, you ask the receptionist for some information.

     ◆ Greet her and ask where the cathedral is.
     ● **Der Dom? Der Dom ist neben dem Rathaus.**
     ◆ Ask if it's far.
     ● **Nein, zehn Minuten zu Fuß.**
     ◆ Now ask where the bank is.
     ● **Gegenüber dem Rathaus.**
     ◆ Thank her and say goodbye.

2   **1•79** Later you ask a man outside the cathedral for help.

     ◆ Ask him where the shopping centre is.
     ● **Das ist nicht weit – geradeaus, die zweite Straße rechts und da ist es.**
     ◆ Ask him to repeat what he said.
     ● **Das ist nicht weit – immer geradeaus, die zweite Straße rechts und da ist es.**
     ◆ Say you don't understand. Ask him to speak more slowly.

3   **1•80** After a break in a café, you decide to go to the tourist office, so you stop a passer-by.

     ◆ Say excuse me and explain that you're a stranger to the town.
     ● **Ja?**
     ◆ Ask where the tourist office is.
     ● **Gehen Sie rechts um die Ecke.**
     ◆ Say thank you and goodbye.

4   **1•81** Outside the tourist office, a stranger asks you where the cathedral is. You've been there, so you can give directions. Say:

     ◆ Go straight ahead.
     ◆ Take the first on the right.
     ◆ The cathedral is on the left, next to the town hall.

quiz

1. If someone says **Das Einkaufszentrum ist da drüben**, what are they telling you?
2. You want to find a chemist's. Which of these phrases do you use? **Wo ist die Post/die Apotheke/der Bahnhof?**
3. How do you tell someone that you don't understand?
4. What directions are you given here? **Gehen Sie geradeaus.**
5. And here? **Nehmen Sie die zweite Straße links.**
6. When would you say **Sprechen Sie langsamer, bitte?**
7. **neben**, **gegenüber**, **nicht weit von** – which means *next to*?
8. **Verkehrsverein**, **Verkehrsamt** – what other word do you know for *tourist information office*?

Now check whether you can ...

- remember the names of places in town
- ask where they are
- understand simple directions
- explain that you are a stranger
- say that you cannot understand
- ask people to repeat information
- ask people to speak more slowly

In several conversations you will have noticed some extra words which occur naturally but don't add essential information: **dann** means *then*, **vielleicht** *perhaps*, **auch** *also*. You probably understood them as you heard them. These 'fillers' help conversation to flow. Why not try using some yourself?

Haben Sie Orangen?

asking for what you want

... and understanding the assistant

buying the quantity you want

dealing with money

In Deutschland ...

in Österreich und in der Schweiz, although there are large supermarkets and department stores, more shopping is done in small specialist shops than in Britain. The market is still an important place for buying fresh produce. Small shops and cafés open early to catch people on their way to work, and bread shops in the suburbs of cities and in small towns and villages supply fresh rolls for breakfast.

Asking for what you want

1 **2•01** Listen to these key phrases.

Haben Sie Orangen?	Have you any oranges?
Was kostet eine Ananas?	How much is a pineapple?
Was kosten die Bananen?	How much are the bananas?
Das ist alles.	That's everything.

2 **2•02** Listen to three people shopping. Note in English what they want.

a ....

b ....

c ....

Auf Deutsch ...

to ask the price of one item, you use **kostet** *costs*: **es kostet vier Euro**; for more than one item, you use **kosten** *cost*: **was kosten die Orangen?** For more on verb patterns like these, see **G8** .

---

3 **2•03** Barbara is at the market, buying fruit for a picnic. Listen and complete her conversation with the stallholder (**Verkäufer**).

Verkäufer	**Bitte schön?**
Barbara	**Was .... die Bananen?**
Verkäufer	**Vier Bananen kosten einen Euro fünfzig (€ 1,50).**
Barbara	**Und .... Sie Orangen?**
Verkäufer	**Ja, hier. Eine Orange .... dreißig Cent (Ct. 30).**
Barbara	**Ich möchte sechs.**
Verkäufer	**Sonst noch etwas?**
Barbara	**Ja, was .... eine Ananas?**
Verkäufer	**Zwei Euro fünfzig (€ 2,50).**
Barbara	**Gut. Vier Bananen, sechs Orangen und eine Ananas, bitte.**

... and understanding the assistant

4   2•04 Listen to these key phrases.

Kann ich Ihnen helfen?	Can I help you?
Die hier?	These here?
... das Stück	... each
... das Kilo	... a kilo

5   2•05 Listen as Barbara does some more shopping. First she buys tomatoes (**Tomaten**) and grapes (**Trauben**), then she goes to the baker's for fresh rolls (**Brötchen**). Number the phrases above as you hear them.

Auf Deutsch ...

the currency in Germany is the euro (**Euro**). 1 Euro = 100 Cent. Note that there is no plural **-s** for **Euro** and **Cent** when used with numbers. You'll hear different ways in which euro amounts are expressed: € 2,40 (*two euros forty cents*) may be either **zwei Euro vierzig** or simply **zwei vierzig**. Note that a comma is used for the decimal point.

---

6   2•05 Now listen to Barbara's conversations again and write the prices in figures. How much does she spend in total?

a   *Verkäufer*   **Guten Tag. Kann ich Ihnen helfen?**
    Barbara   **Ja, ich möchte sechs Tomaten, bitte.**
    Verkäufer   **Sechs Tomaten kosten € ....**
              Sonst noch etwas?
    Barbara   **Ja, und die Trauben.**
    Verkäufer   **Die hier? Gut. Sie kosten € .... das Kilo.**
    Barbara   **Danke.**

b   *Verkäuferin*   **Guten Tag.**
    Barbara   **Guten Tag. Ich möchte Brötchen, bitte.**
              Was kosten sie?
    Verkäuferin   **.................. Cent das Stück.**
    Barbara   **Ich möchte zehn, bitte.**

Buying the quantity you want

1   **2•06** Listen to these words for saying precisely how much you want.

1 kg	**ein Kilo**	**1 l**	**ein Liter**
½ kg	**ein halbes Kilo**	**½ l**	**ein halber Liter**
250 g	**250 Gramm**	**¼ l**	**ein Viertelliter**
100 g	**100 Gramm**		

2   **2•07** Listen to Dieter checking his shopping list and write down the quantity you hear beside each item.

a   .... **Trauben**   c   .... **Rotwein**

b   .... **Milch**   d   .... **Tomaten**

Auf Deutsch ...

there is no word for *of* with quantities and containers:

ein Kilo Trauben	*a kilo of grapes*
ein Glas Bier	*a glass of beer*

---

3   **2•08** Listen to people asking for the following things and number them as you hear them.

eine Dose Tomaten	*a can of tomatoes*	
ein Päckchen Kekse	*a packet of biscuits*	
eine Flasche Orangensaft	*a bottle of orange juice*	
eine Packung Apfelsaft	*a carton of apple juice*	

4   **2•09** Now listen and complete Gerlinde's shopping list.

l ....
    Orangensaft
½ Kg ....
1l ....
l .... Kaffee

6 ....
1 .... Cola
1 Packung ....
.... Tee

Dealing with money

1 **2•10** Listen to these key phrases.

Ich möchte diesen Reisescheck einlösen.	I'd like to cash this traveller's cheque.
Wo kann ich Geld wechseln?	Where can I change money?
Kann ich mit Kreditkarte bezahlen?	Can I pay by credit card?

2 **2•11** Listen to three short conversations and note down in English what each person wants to do.

Manfred ....

Georg ....

Maria ....

Auf Deutsch ...

when saying what you can do or would like to do, the verb expressing this goes to the end:

Wo kann ich Geld wechseln?
literally: *Where can I money to change?*

Ich möchte mit Kreditkarte bezahlen.
literally: *I'd like by credit card to pay.*   **G16**

---

3 Complete these **kann** and **möchte** sentences, using the most suitable verb from the key phrases above.

a **Kann ich hier Geld** ....?

b **Wo kann ich diesen Reisescheck** ....?

c **Ich möchte meine Reiseschecks** ....

put it all together

1 Tick the box(es) in the grid below to indicate the quantities or containers in which you would buy the items on the left. The first one has been done for you.

	250 g	Flasche	Dose	Päckchen	1 Liter
Tee	✓			✓	
Trauben					
Apfelsaft					
Kekse					
Wein					
Cola					

2 To prepare for your shopping trip, put your list into German.

> 1 bottle of orange juice
>
> 1 litre of red wine
>
> ½ kilo of tomatoes
>
> 4 bananas
>
> 1 can of tomatoes
>
> 1 packet of biscuits
>
> 6 rolls

3 Match the two halves of the sentences.

a	Was kosten	Kreditkarte bezahlen?
b	Ich möchte diesen	helfen?
c	Wo kann ich	eine Ananas?
d	Kann ich Ihnen	Reisescheck einlösen.
e	Was kostet	Geld wechseln?
f	Kann ich mit	die Orangen?

You have a busy morning's shopping ahead of you!

1   2•12 At the market: **Auf dem Markt**

The woman at the fruit stall greets you.

- **Tag. Kann ich Ihnen helfen?**
- ◆ Greet the stallholder and ask for 250 grams of grapes and a kilo of bananas.
- **Sonst noch etwas?**
- ◆ You want half a kilo of tomatoes.
- **Gut. Und sonst noch etwas?**
- ◆ Say no, that's all, and thank the stallholder.

2   2•13 At the grocer's: **Im Lebensmittelgeschäft**

- ◆ Ask for six bread rolls.
- **Sonst noch etwas?**
- ◆ Ask how much a packet of biscuits costs.
- **€ 1,50 das Päckchen.**
- ◆ Say you'd like a packet and a bottle of red wine.
- **Sonst noch etwas?**
- ◆ Say yes, you'd like a litre of apple juice.
- **Gut. € 10,80 bitte.**

3   2•14 You go to the bank for more money.

- ◆ Greet the cashier and say you'd like to change some money.
- ◆ When he tells you the amount in euros, say thank you and goodbye.

quiz

1 Would you use **Was kostet ...?** or **Was kosten ...?** to ask the price of: *a* **fünf Brötchen**, *b* **eine Ananas**, *c* **eine Dose Cola**?

2 At the market, how would you ask if they have any tomatoes?

3 How many **Cent** are there in a **Euro**?

4 If **ein Schinkenbrötchen** is a ham roll, how would you ask for a tomato roll?

5 Which word means *to cash*: **wechseln** or **einlösen**?

6 How much wine would you get in a **Viertelliterglas**?

7 If you asked for **zehn Orangen**, what would you expect to get?

8 Would **Apfelsaft** be most likely to come in a **Dose**, a **Packung** or a **Päckchen**?

Now check whether you can ...

- ask how much something costs
- understand the answer
- say that you'd like something
- ask for the quantity you want
- specify the container something comes in
- ask if you can pay by credit card
- say that you want to cash a traveller's cheque or change some money

When going shopping, work out in advance exactly what you want to ask for. This is the point to check words in your dictionary, rather than later on in the shop, when you feel under pressure. You will find it helpful to calculate the quantities and, if possible, anticipate prices and totals. Rehearse your part of the conversation in your mind.

Wo finde ich Geschenke?

finding the right department
in a department store

getting just what you want

understanding opening times

In Deutschland ...

in Österreich und in der Schweiz, you will find at least one department
store (**das Kaufhaus** or **das Warenhaus**) in any large town or city. The
in-store directory will guide you to the appropriate department – **die
Abteilung**. Most shops in Germany, Austria and Switzerland are closed
on Sundays. If you need to make a purchase on a Sunday, you can go to a
railway station, airport or a petrol station. Souvenir shops in tourist areas
are likely to be open on a Sunday too, but generally there is still opposition
to trading by the Church, politicians and trade unions.

Finding the right department

1   2●15 Listen to these key phrases.

Wo finde ich ...	Where can I find ...
... Schreibwaren?	... stationery?
... Geschenke?	... gifts?
Die Geschenkabteilung ist ...	The gift department is ...
... im dritten Stock.	... on the 3rd floor.

Auf Deutsch ...

words are sometimes very long, because they convey ideas which in English would be conveyed by separate words. These compound words become easier to understand and to say if you break them down into their separate parts:

Geschenkabteilung = Geschenk *gift* + Abteilung *department*
Mineralwasser = Mineral *mineral* + Wasser *water*   **G18**

2   **Die Abteilung** *department* can be added to various words:

Sport *sport*	**die Sportabteilung**
Lebensmittel *food*	**die Lebensmittelabteilung**
Süßwaren *confectionery*	**die Süßwarenabteilung**

Can you now write down which department these are sold in?

a   **Schreibwaren** ....
b   **Haushaltswaren** *household goods* ....
c   **Lederwaren** *leather goods* ....

3   2●16 Three customers in a new department store in Berlin ask where to find various departments. Listen and match the department to the floor.

sports department	first floor
leather goods department	second floor
confectionery department	third floor

... in a department store

4 **2•17** Listen to these key phrases.

Wo sind die Toiletten? — Where are the toilets?
Die Toiletten sind ... — The toilets are ...
... im Erdgeschoss. — ... on the ground floor.
Der Parkplatz ist ... — The car park is ...
... im Untergeschoss. — ... in the basement.

Auf Deutsch ...

in the is **in dem** with **der** and **das** words and **in der** with **die** words.

In dem is usually shortened to **im**, as in **im Erdgeschoss**.
In der is not shortened: **in der Geschenkabteilung**. **G6**

---

5 **2•18** Karen, an assistant in the store, is explaining where some of the store's services are. Listen and decide whether the statements below are true (**richtig**) or false (**falsch**). You should recognise the German for *restaurant* without difficulty.

	Richtig	Falsch
a The car park is on the ground floor.		
b The toilets are on the first floor.		
c The restaurant is in the basement.		

6 **2•19** Listen as Karen gives each customer – **Kunde** (m) or **Kundin** (f) – directions. Complete their conversations.

a *Kunde* **Entschuldigen Sie. Wo .... die Toiletten?**
  Karen **Die Toiletten? Sie sind ....,
  neben dem Parkplatz.**

b *Kunde* **Wo .... das Restaurant?**
  Karen **Gegenüber der Bank ....**

c *Kundin* **Wo finde ich Geschenke?**
  Karen **Die Geschenkabteilung ist ....**

Getting just what you want

1 **2•20** Listen to these key phrases.

Ich suche ein T-Shirt.	I'm looking for a T-shirt.
Das ist zu groß/zu klein.	That's too big/too small.
Die sind zu teuer.	Those are too expensive.
Das ist schön.	That's nice.
Ich nehme ein T-Shirt.	I'll take a T-shirt.

eine Flasche Wein   Pralinen   eine Tasche

2   **2•21** Listen to three conversations in a department store and note down in English what each customer wants to buy. Then listen again and note what is said about it (e.g. *nice/too small*). You'll also hear the useful little word **aber**, meaning *but*.

	Article	Comments
a		
b		
c		

3   **2•22** Kerstin is doing some shopping, but there is a problem with some of the things she is offered. Listen and tick what you think she will buy.

T-shirt   wine   bag   chocolates

4   How would you say:

- That's too big?
- I'll take a bottle of wine?
- I'm looking for a bag?

Understanding opening times

1   2•23 Listen to these key phrases.

Wann sind Sie geöffnet?	When are you open?
Wir sind ...	We are ...
... von 9 bis 6 geöffnet.	... open from 9 a.m. to 6 p.m.
... samstags geschlossen.	... closed on Saturdays.
Montag ist Ruhetag.	Monday is our day off./ We're closed on Mondays.

Montag *Mon*		**Donnerstag** *Thurs*	
Dienstag *Tue*		**Freitag** *Fri*	
Mittwoch *Wed*		**Samstag** *Sat*	
		Sonntag *Sun*	

Auf Deutsch ...

adding **-s** to any day of the week turns it into *on -days*:

Montag	*Monday*	**montags**	*on Mondays*
Samstag	*Saturday*	**samstags**	*on Saturdays*

Sonnabend is an alternative word for Saturday used in some areas.

2   Which store is open every day from Monday to Friday?

a   mittwochs Ruhetag

b   **SAMSTAGS GESCHLOSSEN**

c   Dienstag Ruhetag

3   2•24 Kerstin is planning her shopping trip and checks the opening times of the local stores. Listen and note down in English the hours when the stores are open and which day each is closed.

a   ....

b   ....

c   ....

put it all together

1   What do these notices say?

a

> Dienstags
> Ruhetag

b

> **Toiletten im
> Untergeschoss**

c

> **Geöffnet von
> 8 bis 12 und
> von 2 bis 7**

d

> Restaurant
> bis Donnerstag
> geschlossen

2   Reorder a to e to form a conversation between a shop
assistant and a customer.

a   **Ja, das ist schön. Ich nehme ein T-Shirt.** ....
b   **Ich suche ein Geschenk.**   ....
c   **Oder ein T-Shirt?**   ....
d   **Vielleicht eine Tasche?**   ....
e   **Das ist zu teuer.**   ....

3   Match the German to the English.

a	**teuer**	big
b	**groß**	nice
c	**schön**	small
d	**klein**	expensive

4   Where would you find these items? Match them to the right
department.

a	**Tasche**	**Lebensmittelabteilung**
b	**Pralinen**	**Haushaltswarenabteilung**
c	**Brötchen**	**Süßwarenabteilung**
d	**Tasse**	**Lederwarenabteilung**

now you're talking!

You're shopping in a big Hamburg department store.

1   2•25   You approach an assistant to ask for help.

   ◆ Ask where the toilets are.
   ● **Die Toiletten sind im zweiten Stock.**
   ◆ Say thanks and ask where you can find the sports department.
   ● **Im Erdgeschoss.**
   ◆ You've just been there to buy food. Ask if it's next to the food hall.
   ● **Ja, neben der Lebensmittelabteilung.**

2   2•26   You make your way to the gift department.

   ◆ Tell the assistant you're looking for presents.
   ● **Vielleicht Pralinen?**
   ◆ Say those are too expensive (you've seen the price!).
   ● **Eine Tasche? Oder eine Flasche Wein?**
   ◆ Ask how much a bag costs.
   ● **€ 25.**
   ◆ Say good, you'll take a bag.

3   2•27   You've done enough shopping for today; perhaps you'll come back tomorrow in the car.

   ◆ Ask when the store is open.
   ● **Wir sind von 9 bis 6 geöffnet. Montag ist Ruhetag.**
   ◆ Ask where the car park is.
   ● **Im Untergeschoss, neben der Haushaltswarenabteilung.**
   ◆ Say thank you and goodbye.

quiz

1 Which day follows **Dienstag**?
2 Which is the odd one out: **groß**, **teuer**, **geöffnet**, **schön**?
3 Where in a department store can you get something to eat: **im Parkplatz**, **im Restaurant** or **in der Lebensmittelabteilung**?
4 What is the assistant telling you? **Wir sind mittwochs geschlossen.**
5 What are the two words for *Saturday*?
6 Which means *basement*: **Erdgeschoss** or **Untergeschoss**?
7 **Das T-Shirt ist zu groß, die Tasche ist zu klein.** Which item is too big?
8 In which department would you find writing paper?

Now check whether you can ...

- find your way to various departments in a store
  ... and the different floors in a building
- describe what you want
- say why something is or isn't suitable
- say you will take something
- ask when a store is open
  ... and understand opening and closing times
- recognise the days of the week

Remember that a lot of spoken communication is accompanied by gesture and body language. If you don't know the word for the item you want, for example, point to it on the shelf or rail. If you have forgotten how to say that the fit or size is wrong, indicate it with your arms. To be a successful communicator you have to be a bit of a performer. Go ahead and try – you've nothing to lose!

Kontrollpunkt 2

1 Match the German and the English.

a	die Apotheke	the tourist information office
b	der Bahnhof	left
c	erste Straße rechts	on the third floor
d	das Verkehrsamt	straight ahead
e	geradeaus	the station
f	im dritten Stock	in the stationery department
g	das Restaurant	the chemist's
h	gegenüber	the restaurant
i	links	opposite
j	in der Schreibwaren-abteilung	first road on the right

2 Complete the crossword by putting these words from your shopping list into German.

1 coke
2 coffee
3 biscuits
4 pineapple
5 oranges
6 apple juice
7 bottle
8 bananas
9 can
10 wine
11 tomatoes
12 grapes

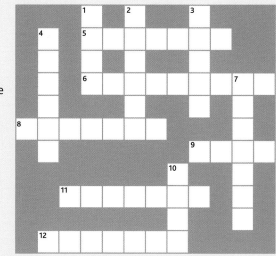

3   Helga has made a shopping list too, but has forgotten to note down
    the quantities. Choose the most suitable word or phrase on the left to
    go with each item.

ein Päckchen
sechs Dosen
eine Flasche
eine
ein halbes Kilo
fünf

.... Ananas
.... Cola
.... Trauben
.... Kaffee
.... Orangen
.... Weißwein

4   **2•28** Listen to some phrases overheard in a department store and
    check whether the prices you hear are the same as the ones on the
    tags. Tick the correct ones and change the ones that are wrong.

a   € 7,00   d   € 14,20   f   € 4,50

b   € 76,50   e   € 14,00   g   €46,00

c   € 3,20

5   **2•29** Frau Braun and Herr Martin are shopping at the local store.
    Listen and write down what each one buys and the amount they pay.

Frau Braun   ....
                    ....

Herr Martin   ....
                    ....

6   **2•30** Three tourists in Munich all ask the way from the market place
    to the cathedral. Listen to the replies they receive and look at the map
    on the next page. Which of the three would get to the cathedral, and
    where would the other two end up?

a   ....
b   ....
c   ....

7   Here is part of the store guide (**Wegweiser**) to a large department store.

WEGWEISER	
3. Stock	**Bank** **Restaurant**
2. Stock	**Lederwaren**
1. Stock	**Geschenkabteilung**
Erdgeschoss	**Schreibwaren**
Untergeschoss	**Süßwaren** **Lebensmittel**

Which floor do you need:

a   to buy your brother a birthday present?   ....

b   to buy a handbag?   ....

c   to change some money?   ....

d   to buy some envelopes?   ....

e   to buy some sweets for the children?   ....

8 Below is a plan of the third floor of the store. Complete the directions.

a **Die Bank ist gegenüber** ....

b **Die Bank ist neben** ....

c **Die Toiletten** .... **der Sportabteilung.**

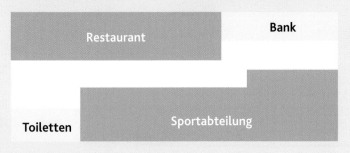

| Restaurant | Bank |
| Toiletten | Sportabteilung |

9 Martin has written to a friend, describing his working day. Read the extract from his letter and tick the true statements below.

> **Büro** *office*
> **ich arbeite** *I work*
> **Mittagspause** *midday break*

> Ich habe einen Parkplatz im Untergeschoss und mein Büro ist im dritten Stock. Die Sekretärin, Frau Schwarz, hat ein Büro im zweiten Stock. Ich arbeite von neun bis eins und von zwei bis sechs. Ich habe von eins bis zwei Mittagspause. Gegenüber dem Büro ist ein Warenhaus. Das Restaurant da ist gut; es ist dienstags bis freitags geöffnet. Montags ist Ruhetag und ich gehe zum Café um die Ecke. Es ist nicht weit.

a Martin parks his car in the basement.

b Martin's office is on the 3rd floor.

c Frau Schwarz also works in the same office.

d Martin gets an hour and a half for his midday break.

e He usually eats in the restaurant in the department store opposite.

f On Mondays he goes to a café which is quite far away.

Ich möchte ein Zimmer

checking in at reception

asking for a hotel room

booking ahead

enquiring about facilities

In Deutschland …

in Österreich und in der Schweiz, a wide range of accommodation is available. Standards are high and prices can be moderate. The best place for help and advice is the tourist office (**Touristinfo**), or you can look at the lists of accommodation (**Zimmernachweis**) displayed in public places.

The sign ZIMMER FREI means that rooms are available. There is no all-purpose phrase for *no vacancies*, but the most common expression is **voll besetzt**.

Many English-speaking people assume that a **Gasthaus** is a guest house, whereas it is in fact a pub!

Checking in at reception

1   2•31 Listen to these key phrases.

Ich habe eine Reservierung für ...	I've booked ...
... ein Einzelzimmer ...	... a single room ...
... ein Doppelzimmer ...	... a double room ...
... mit Dusche.	... with a shower ...
... mit Bad.	... with a bath.
Hier ist der Schlüssel.	Here's the key.

2   2•32 Listen as the receptionist at the Hotel Sonne greets the guests and checks their names in the register. Tick the relevant boxes in the grid and note the room number in the last column.

	Doppelzimmer	Einzelzimmer	Bad	Dusche	Nummer
Friedmann					
Wolf					
Lange					

> **Auf Deutsch ...**
>
> **nicht wahr?** and **ja?** are used to check that what you have just said is correct, just as English speakers use *isn't it?*, *don't you?* and so on. The word **oder?** can be used in the same way.

3   2•33 Listen to three more people checking in. This time, note the type of room each has reserved and the floor they are on.

a *Dürnbeck*   ....
b *Auerbach*   ....
c *Meyer*   ....

Which person did you hear being asked their name?

Asking for a hotel room

1   **2•34** Listen to these key phrases.

Haben Sie ein Zimmer frei?	Do you have a room (vacant)?
Für wie lange?	For how long?
Für heute.	For tonight.
Für zwei Nächte.	For two nights.
Wie schreibt man das?	How do you spell that?

2   **2•35** Listen to three people enquiring about hotel rooms. How long does each one want to stay?

a   ....   b   c   ....

3   **2•36** Listen to Kurt saying the German alphabet:

A B C D E F G H I J K L M N O P Q R S T U V W X Y Z Ä Ö Ü

Now listen as he spells his own name. His **Vorname** *first name* is **Kurt**. What is his **Familienname** *surname*?

> **Familienname:** ....
> **Vorname:**   *Kurt* ....

4   **2•37** Listen to the rest of the receptionist's conversation with the three guests in activity 2. Write their names as they spell them.

a   ....   b   c   ....

Now practise spelling your own name.

5   How would you say:

- Do you have a room for tonight?
- A single room for four nights, please.
- Do you have a double room for three nights?

Booking ahead

1   **2•38** Listen to these key phrases.

Ich möchte ein Zimmer reservieren.	I'd like to book a room.
Für wann?	When for?
Vom zweiten ...	From the second ...
... bis zum vierten.	... until the fourth.
Es tut mir leid ...	I'm sorry ...
... das Hotel ist voll besetzt.	... the hotel is full.

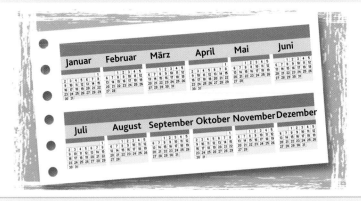

Auf Deutsch ...

you use *first*, *second*, *third*, etc. both to give dates and to say what floor something is on.

From 1st to 19th you add **-ten** to the number:

    zwei + ten = zweiten *2nd*; vier + ten = vierten *4th*

There are four exceptions:

    ersten *1st*, **dritten** *3rd*, **siebten** *7th*, **achten** *8th*

From 20th onwards, you add **-sten** instead:

    vierundzwanzig + sten = vierundzwanzigsten *24th*

The abbreviated form uses a full stop: **1.** = *1st*, **2.** = *2nd*, and so on.

2   **2•39** Listen to the receptionist at the Hotel Sonne taking bookings over the phone. What dates are the rooms wanted for?

a ....   b ....   c ....

Which customer will be disappointed?

Enquiring about facilities

1   **2•40** Listen to these key phrases.

Gibt es ein Schwimmbad?	Is there a swimming pool?
Gibt es eine Bank in der Nähe?	Is there a bank nearby?
Es gibt einen Parkplatz.	There is a car park.
Wann ist Frühstück?	When is breakfast?
Bis wann ist die Bar geöffnet?	Until when is the bar open?

2   **2•41** Listen as some guests make enquiries at the reception desk and note in English what each person asks.

a ....

b ....

c ....

d ....

3   **2•41** Listen again and write the information they receive next to their question above. **Hinter dem Hotel** means *behind the hotel*.

Auf Deutsch ...

    es gibt means both *there is* and *there are*.

    gibt es? means both *is there?* and *are there?*

---

4   **2•42** Brigitte is telling her tour party about the Hotel Sonne. Listen and note the information in English. **Abends** is, of course, *in the evening*.

a   breakfast times   ....

b   restaurant hours   ....

c   location of bar   ....

d   location of swimming pool   ....

Listen again: how long will the party be staying?

put it all together

1   Read the memo about Hans Kraus, who is visiting a German
    company. Fill in the hotel form for him; you should be able to
    guess what the unfamiliar words mean.

> Hans Kraus ist Architekt. Er ist im Hotel Bach
> in Leipzig vom elften bis zum achtzehnten
> September. Er hat Zimmer Nummer
> sechsundsiebzig. Herr Kraus ist Holländer.

HOTEL BACH

Familienname:.................... Vorname: ....

Beruf:.................... Nationalität: ....

Zimmernummer: .... vom: .... bis zum: ....

2   Complete the sentences with the help of the symbols.

a   **Ich habe eine Reservierung
    für** ....

b   **Gibt es** ....?

c   **Wann ist** ....?

d   **Ich habe eine Reservierung
    vom** ....

    `1 / 3 - 4 / 3`

3   Match the German to the English.

a	**Für wann?**	For how long?
b	**Haben Sie ein Zimmer frei?**	nearby
c	**Das Hotel ist voll besetzt.**	behind the hotel
d	**in der Nähe**	When for?
e	**hinter dem Hotel**	The hotel's full.
f	**Für wie lange?**	Do you have a room?

now you're talking!

1   2•43 Take the part of Hannelore Förster, arriving at the Hotel Ludwig.

- **Guten Tag. Kann ich Ihnen helfen?**
- ◆ Greet the receptionist and ask if they have a room.
- **Ein Einzelzimmer oder ein Doppelzimmer?**
- ◆ Say a single room with a bathroom.
- **Für wie lange?**
- ◆ Say for three nights.
- **Gut. Also Zimmer dreiundneunzig im zweiten Stock.**

2   2•44 Now take the part of this hotel guest.

- ◆ Greet the receptionist and say you've booked a room.
- **Wie heißen Sie?**
- ◆ Give your name.
- **Ein Doppelzimmer mit Dusche, nicht wahr?**
- ◆ Say yes, and when you want it for.
- **Gut. Hier ist der Schlüssel, Herr Wilson.**
- ◆ Ask if there's a car park nearby.
- **Ja, hinter dem Hotel.**

> James Wilson
>
> Hotel zum Goldenen Löwen
>
> Double room with shower
>
> 19/6–26/6

3   2•45 This time you ring the Eurotel to book a room.

- **Guten Morgen. Eurotel Dresden.**
- ◆ Say good morning, you'd like to book a room.
- **Für wann?**
- ◆ Say for tonight.
- **Für wie lange?**
- ◆ Say until the twelfth.
- **Ja, wie heißen Sie, bitte?**
- ◆ Say your name.
- **Wie schreibt man das?**
- ◆ Give the information.

quiz

1. Which month follows **Februar**?
2. Write down the dates you are staying: **vom dritten bis zum neunten Mai**.
3. What information do you want if you ask **Wann ist Frühstück?**
4. How would you ask: *Is there a swimming pool nearby?*
5. Which is your surname: **Vorname** or **Familienname**?
6. If someone says **für fünf Nächte**, how long are they staying?
7. What do you do if someone asks **Wie schreibt man das?**
8. If someone says **Es tut mir leid**, are they expressing pleasure, regret or anger?

Now check whether you can ...

- say that you've booked a room
- ask if a room is available
- book a room by phone
- specify the kind of room you want
- say how long you want the room for and give precise dates
- spell your name in German
- understand the spelling of other people's names
- ask about hotel facilities

Before you listen to or take part in a recorded conversation, imagine yourself in that situation. What would you say if you were in a hotel in England, for example? This helps you to anticipate what people will say in German and makes it easier to understand what you hear.

Wann fährt der nächste Zug?

asking about public transport

... and arrival and departure times

buying tickets and checking travel details

In Deutschland ...

in Österreich und in der Schweiz, public transport is generally clean, quick and reliable. In many cities there is a wide variety of means of transport: you can travel **mit der Straßenbahn** *by tram*, **mit dem Bus** *by bus* or **mit der U-Bahn** *by underground*. Most towns and cities have an integrated transport system, where one ticket is valid for all forms of public transport within the city limits. Tickets can be bought in advance and should be validated (punched) with the date on the bus or tram, or at a railway station. In many places you can also travel on local waterways, **mit der Fähre** *by ferry* or **mit dem Dampfer** *by steamer*.

Asking about public transport

1   **2•46** Listen to these key phrases.

Wo ist die Bushaltestelle?	Where is the bus stop?
Fährt diese Straßenbahn ...	Does this tram go ...
Welche Linie fährt ...	Which number/line goes ...
... zum Stadion?	... to the stadium?
... zur Stadtmitte?	... to the town centre?
... nach Garmisch?	... to Garmisch?

2   **2•47** Listen to various people in **München** *Munich* asking how to get to places by tram, and complete the grid below.

	a	b	c	d
Number	5			
Place			Schwabing	station

Auf Deutsch ...

nach is used for *to* with names of towns and cities:

nach Hamburg, nach Boston

zu is used if you're travelling to other places and its ending varies according to the gender (**der, die, das**) of the word:

zum Bahnhof (der), zur Apotheke (die), zum Rathaus (das)

---

3   **2•48** Listen to the conversation in a Munich street and fill the gaps below. Where does the visitor (**Besucher**) want to go, and how will he get there?

Besucher   **Fährt diese .... zum Rathaus, bitte?**
Frau   **Nein, ... Schwabing. Der Bus .... zum Rathaus. Dort drüben ist die ....**
Besucher   **Welche .... fährt .... Rathaus?**
Frau   **Die .... fünf.**

... and arrival and departure times

4 2•49 Listen to these key phrases.

Wann fährt der nächste Zug?	When does the next train go?
Der Zug nach Berlin ...	The train to Berlin ...
... fährt um sieben Uhr.	... goes at seven o'clock.
Wann kommt der Zug in Bonn an?	When does the train arrive in Bonn?
Um dreizehn Uhr dreißig.	At 13:30.

5 2•50 Listen to the announcements at Linz's main station and make a note of the times of the arrivals and departures.

	Abfahrt *Departure*	**Ankunft** *Arrival*
Siegen		
Linz		
Zürich		
Leipzig		

Auf Deutsch ...

certain verbs, like **ankommen** *to arrive*, can split into two parts: **an** and **kommen**. An goes at the end of the sentence: **Wann kommt der Zug/Bus in ... an?** Don't forget to include it!   **G17**

---

6 2•51 In the Munich tourist office, people are asking about transport. Listen and complete the grid in English.

Place	Time	Transport
Garmisch		
Schwabing		
Stadium		
Town centre		

Buying tickets

1   **2•52** Listen to these key phrases.

Einmal nach München.	One (ticket) to Munich.
Einfach ...	Single ...
... oder hin und zurück?	... or return?
zweimal erster Klasse	two first class (tickets)
dreimal zweiter Klasse	three second class (tickets)

Auf Deutsch ...

the word for ticket (**Fahrkarte**) is not normally used when actually buying one. Instead, **-mal** is added to the number of tickets needed: **einmal zweiter Klasse einfach nach Berlin**. The pattern 'number, class, type, destination' is a useful one to learn.

2   **2•53** There's a queue of people buying train tickets at **Köln** *Cologne* station. Listen: how many do they want? First or second class? Write the numbers in the grid. Then listen again: what type of ticket do they ask for?

Destination	Number	Class	Type
Innsbruck			
Potsdam			
Augsburg			
Vaduz			
Basel			

3   How would you ask for these tickets? (Remember the pattern.)

- single tickets for two people first class to Munich
- a return ticket to Innsbruck for one person, second class
- four second class singles to Mainz
- three returns to Mannheim, second class

... and checking travel details

4   2•54 Listen to these key phrases.

Muss ich umsteigen?	Do I have to change?
Wo muss ich aussteigen?	Where must I get off?
Kann ich einen Platz reservieren?	Can I reserve a seat?
Von welchem Gleis fährt der Zug?	Which platform does the train go from?

5   2•55 Listen to the travellers making enquiries at the Cologne booking office and note down where each person wants to go. Listen again and note what additional information they ask for. (The employee's **Ja, sicher** means *Yes, of course*.)

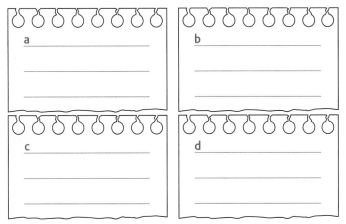

6   Find the appropriate response to each question.

a	**Muss ich umsteigen?**	**Von Gleis 7.**
b	**Kann ich einen Platz reservieren?**	**In Berlin.**
c	**Von welchem Gleis fährt der Zug?**	**Ja, sicher.**
d	**Wo muss ich aussteigen?**	**Ja, in Köln.**

7   What questions would you ask to find out:
   - if you need to change?
   - what platform the train leaves from?
   - where to get off?

put it all together

1   Two conversations have got mixed up. Recreate them by numbering the sentences A 1 to 4 and B 1 to 4.

Conversation A: **Buying a ticket**

Conversation B: **At the bus stop**

....   **Und wo ist die Bushaltestelle für die Linie 7?**
....   **Nach Bonn? Ja, einfach oder hin und zurück?**
....   **Die Linie 7 zur Stadtmitte? Um 17:00.**
....   **Da drüben, gegenüber dem Rathaus.**
....   **€ 28,40 einmal einfach nach Bonn.**
..B.. ..1..   **Wann fährt der Bus zur Stadtmitte, bitte?**
..A.. ..1..   **Einmal nach Bonn, bitte.**
....   **Einfach, bitte.**

2   Practise saying the following times and then write them out in words.

a 14:40   b 16:30   c 12:05   d 07:15

3   Fill in the appropriate question words.

a   **Von .... Gleis fährt der Zug? Von Gleis 3.**
b   **............... fährt der Zug nach Berlin? Um 12:30.**
c   **............... ist die Straßenbahnhaltestelle? Dort drüben.**
d   **............... Linie fährt zum Stadion? Die Linie 8.**
e   **............... muss ich umsteigen? In Berlin.**

4   Complete these sentences with the correct word for *to*.

a   **Mein Mann fährt heute .... Innsbruck.**
b   **Die Straßenbahn fährt .... Stadtmitte.**
c   **Welche Linie fährt .... Stadion?**
d   **Der Zug fährt .... München.**

1   **2•56** You're staying in Munich and want to make an outing to Bad Tölz by train. You go to the main station (**der Hauptbahnhof**) and hear this announcement.

- **Der nächste Zug nach Bad Tölz fährt in** .... **von** .... **ab.**

You didn't catch the details, so you go to the ticket office.
- ◆ Ask when the train leaves.
- **In zwanzig Minuten, um 13:25.**
- ◆ Ask which platform it leaves from.
- **Von Gleis vier.**
- ◆ Ask for a second class return ticket.

2   **2•57** While you wait, you go to the advance booking office to get the ticket for your trip to Hamburg.

- ◆ Say you want a single second class ticket to Hamburg.
- **Nach Hamburg?**
- ◆ Say yes and ask how much it costs.
- **Es kostet € 90.**
- ◆ Ask if you can reserve a seat.
- **Ja, sicher.**

3   **2•58** You also want to visit the **Stadttheater** in Oberammergau. Prepare what you need to ask, using the notes below, then take part in the conversation on the audio. You want to know:

- ◆ where the bus stop is
- ◆ what a return ticket costs
- ◆ the time of the next bus
- ◆ the time of arrival in Oberammergau
- ◆ where you have to get off
- ◆ if it's far to the Stadttheater
- ◆ when the bus back to Munich leaves.

quiz

1 You are told **Sie müssen in Koblenz umsteigen.** What must you do?

2 You hear **von Gleis zwölf** – are you at the railway station or the bus stop?

3 What is the German for *bus route/number*?

4 How do you say *to the station*?

5 What do you know about this train? **der Zug nach Bonn**

6 Which board tells you about arrivals: the one headed **Ankunft** or **Abfahrt**?

7 How do you say *by tram*: **mit der U-Bahn**, **mit der Fähre** or **mit der Straßenbahn**?

8 How do you ask about reserving a seat? **Kann ich ....
reservieren?**

Now check whether you can ...

- ask about transport to places in town
- ask about transport to other towns and cities
- ask about arrival and departure times
- ask for single and return tickets
- ask if you can book a seat
- ask whether you have to change
- ask where to get off
- understand straightforward replies to all these questions

There are often several ways of saying the same thing, so it's a good idea in the early stages to learn the patterns given in the units even if you then hear other expressions being used. As you progress and gain confidence you can, of course, begin to experiment with other patterns.

Guten Appetit!

reading the menu

ordering a meal

choosing cakes and desserts

finishing the meal

In Deutschland ...

in Österreich und in der Schweiz, the quality and variety of food is generally good. In every region you will find many local specialities (**Spezialitäten**) and different types of bread, beer, sausage (**Wurst**), ham (**Schinken**) and cheese (**Käse**). Cakes and gateaux are popular everywhere as desserts, and are also enjoyed with coffee at other times of the day. A visit to the **Konditorei** (cake shop, usually with café) is to be recommended.

In German households the main meal of the day still tends to be at midday, and the evening meal often consists of soup (**Suppe**) or cold meats (**Aufschnitt**). Both at home and when eating out, it is customary to begin the meal by saying **Guten Appetit!** *Enjoy your meal*!

Reading the menu

1 **2●59** Listen to these key phrases.

Die Speisekarte, bitte.	The menu, please.
Was ist ... ?	What is ...?
Was für Fleisch ist das?	What kind of meat is it?
Ist das Rindfleisch?	Is it beef?
Ist das Schweinefleisch ...	Is it pork ...
... oder Kalbfleisch?	... or veal?

2 **2●60** Three people at the Restaurant Alpenblick are asking about unfamiliar dishes. Listen and note the type of meat they contain.

Sauerbraten ....

Weißwurst ....

Jägerschnitzel ....

3 The secret of understanding a menu is to home in on the words you think you recognise and make inspired guesses! Look at these starters (**Vorspeisen**) and main courses (**Hauptgerichte**) and decide what each dish contains. If in doubt, check with the glossary.

SPEISEKARTE *Restaurant Alpenblick*

VORSPEISEN
a **Heringssalat**
b **Krabbencocktail**
c **Melone mit Schinken**

HAUPTGERICHTE
d **Rumpsteak**
e **Kalbsleber**
f **Schweinekotelett**
g **Rinderbraten**
h **Großer Salat mit Tunfisch**

Ordering a meal

1   **2•61** Listen to these key phrases.

Was ist die Tagessuppe?	What is the soup of the day?
Was empfehlen Sie?	What do you recommend?
Das Hähnchen ist gut.	The chicken is good.
Und zum Trinken …?	And to drink …?

2   **2•62** Listen as Helga and Kurt order a meal from the waitress
(**Kellnerin**) and fill the gaps. Listen out for **also**, one of those filler
words, meaning *in that case*. What do you think **Salat** is?

Kellnerin **Bitte schön?**
Helga   **Was .... Sie?**
Kellnerin **Der Sauerbraten und das Hähnchen mit Salat sind**

....
Helga   **Ich nehme das Hähnchen.**
Kurt   **Und was ist die ....?**
Kellnerin **Tomatensuppe.**
Kurt   **Also eine Tomatensuppe und zwei Hähnchen.**

3   **2•63** Helga and Kurt are still talking to the waitress. Listen and note
down in English what each orders.

Helga   ....
Kurt   ....

4   **2•64** Three other customers at the Alpenblick restaurant are deciding
what to order. Listen to their conversations and answer the questions.

- Which customer – *a*, *b* or *c* – asks for a recommendation?
- How many of them have starters?
- What is the pork chop served with?
- Who has fish followed by chicken?
- Do they order chicken with rice (**Reis**) or chips (**Pommes frites**)?

Choosing cakes and desserts

1   **2•65** Listen to these key phrases.

Als Nachspeise nehme ich ...   For dessert I'll have ...
... gemischtes Eis.   ... mixed ice cream.
... ein Stück Nusstorte.   ... a piece of nut gateau.
Wir haben frisches Obst.   We have fresh fruit.

2   **2•66** Two customers are looking
at the Alpenblick's dessert menu.
Listen to their conversation and
tick the items they choose. Before
listening, look up the two new
words in the glossary.

NACHSPEISEN
Käsekuchen
Nusstorte
Schokoladentorte
gemischtes Eis mit Sahne
frisches Obst

3   **2•67** Listen to a customer in the Konditorei Ralf ordering for herself
and two friends. Which of the three orders below is hers?

a

1 nut gateau
1 chocolate ice
   cream with cream
1 chocolate cake
3 coffees

b

1 nut gateau with
   cream
1 chocolate cake
   with cream
1 fruit gateau
3 coffees

c

1 fruit gateau
1 nut gateau
   with cream
1 chocolate cake
3 coffees

Finishing the meal

1   **2•68** Listen to these key phrases.

Hat's geschmeckt?	Did you enjoy your meal?
Ja, es hat gut geschmeckt.	Yes, it was good.
Die Rechnung, bitte.	The bill, please.
Das macht € 54,70.	That comes to € 54.70.
Zahlen Sie bitte an der Kasse.	Please pay at the cash desk.
Das ist für Sie.	Here's something for you.

2   **2•69** Helga and Kurt have finished their meal and call the waitress over to their table. Listen to the conversation.

   a   What did they have for dessert?
   b   Where do they pay?
   c   Do they leave a tip?
   d   Which of the following is their bill?

   € 73,20   € 27,30   € 23,70   € 72,30

3   **2•70** Listen to the customer at the next table and fill the blanks in his conversation with the waitress below. What is he asking when he says **Was macht das?**

Mann   **Die ...., bitte.**
Fräulein **Ja, gut. Hat's ....?**
Mann   **Ja, es hat .... Was macht das?**
Fräulein **Das .... € 36.**
Mann   **Danke. Das ist ....**

4   What would you say:

   ● when you want the bill?
   ● when you give a tip?
   ● when you have enjoyed your meal?

put it all together

1 Put the following items in the right place on the menu.

Vorspeisen	Hauptgerichte	Nachspeisen

Schweinekotelett	Heringssalat	Tomatensuppe
Käsekuchen	Hähnchen	Kalbsleber
gemischtes Eis	Rinderbraten	Tunfischsalat
Apfelkuchen	frisches Obst	

2 Number the sentences in the correct order to make a conversation between a customer and a waitress.

a Das ist Kalbfleisch.   ....

b Ein Glas Apfelsaft.   ....

c Bitte schön.   ....

d Gut, also Schnitzel mit Pommes frites, bitte.   ....

e Die Speisekarte, bitte.   ....

f Und zum Trinken?   ....

g Wiener Schnitzel – was für Fleisch ist das?   ....

3 Find the appropriate response to each of a to f.

a	Und zum Trinken?	Das ist Kalbfleisch.
b	Und als Nachspeise?	Einen Viertelliter Weißwein, bitte.
c	Hat's geschmeckt?	Der Fisch ist gut.
d	Was macht das?	Ich nehme gemischtes Eis.
e	Was empfehlen Sie?	Es hat gut geschmeckt.
f	Was ist Weißwurst?	€ 45,20.

1 **2•71** You arrive in a restaurant and take a seat.

- ◆ Ask for the menu.
- ● **Bitte schön.**
- ◆ Point to an unfamiliar item (**Eisbein**). Ask what type of meat it is.
- ● **Eisbein – das ist Schweinefleisch.**
- ◆ You don't like pork; order chicken with rice.
- ● **Und zum Trinken?**
- ◆ Ask for a glass of mineral water.

2 **2•72** On another occasion you find it difficult to choose.

- ◆ Ask what they recommend.
- ● **Der Fisch ist heute sehr frisch.**
- ◆ Say good, in that case the fish please.
- ● **Mit Salat oder Pommes frites?**
- ◆ Say you would like salad.

3 **2•73** When the waitress brings the meal, she wishes you

- ● **Guten Appetit!**

Later she returns and asks:
- ● **Hat's geschmeckt?**
- ◆ Say yes, and as dessert you'll have fresh fruit.
- ● **Und sonst noch etwas?**
- ◆ Say you'd like a pot of coffee with cream.

4 **2•74** Now you've finished your meal.

- ◆ Say you want the bill.
- ● **Also ... Fisch mit Salat, frisches Obst und ein Kännchen Kaffee ... Das macht €13,60.**

As you are about to offer her the money, she says
- ● **Zahlen Sie bitte an der Kasse.**
- ◆ Offer her a tip.
- ● **Danke schön. Auf Wiedersehen.**

quiz

1 Which is the odd one out: **Rinderbraten**, **Rumpsteak** or **Schweinekotelett**?

2 What do you say to people as they start their meal?

3 In what order do these appear on a menu? **Hauptgerichte**, **Nachspeisen**, **Vorspeisen**

4 Which is made of veal: **Jägerschnitzel** or **Wiener Schnitzel**?

5 How do you tell someone the meal was good?

6 Which of these would you choose if you were a vegetarian: **Hähnchen**, **Tomatensuppe** or **Schinken**?

7 You go to the **Kasse** – what do you do there?

8 When do you say **Das ist für Sie**?

Now check whether you can ...

- work out what the main items on a menu are
- ask about items on the menu
- order a meal with drinks
- say that you enjoyed your meal
- ask for the bill
- offer the waiter/waitress a tip

Before going out to eat in a German restaurant, it's a good idea to look up in the dictionary any food or drink you don't like, such as liver (**Leber**), kidneys (**Nieren**), onions (**Zwiebeln**), or garlic (**Knoblauch**). That way you can avoid disappointments!

And now, congratulations on reaching the end of **Talk German**. Prepare yourself for the final **Kontrollpunkt** with some revision. Listen to the conversations again – the more you listen the more confident you will become – and use the quizzes and checklists to assess how much you can remember. And take every opportunity to speak German; if no one else is available, talk aloud to yourself!

Kontrollpunkt 3

You've arrived in a small South German town at the start of your holiday.

1 You take a taxi to your hotel, the Hotel Adler, and talk to Maria, the receptionist. Fill the gaps in your conversation with the appropriate word or phrase from the box.

You	**Guten Abend. Ich habe eine ....**
Maria	**Wie .... , bitte?**
You	**Mein .... ist ....**
Maria	**Ach ja, ein Einzelzimmer mit Bad, nicht wahr?**
You	**Nein, nein, ein Einzelzimmer ....**
Maria	**Oh, entschuldigen Sie, und bis wann?**
You	**Bis ....**

> mit Dusche
> Reservierung
> zum neunten
> Name
> heißen Sie
> your name

2 2•75 Once in your room, you decide to ring reception for some information. Work out how you will ask the following, then listen to check your questions and note down the information given.

a When is breakfast?   ....
b Where is the bar?   ....
c When is the bar open?   ....
d Is there a swimming pool in the hotel? ....

3 Next day you want to go on a day trip by ferry across the lake to Konstanz. You ask for details at reception. For each question choose the correct options.

a **Wann fährt die U-Bahn/die Straßenbahn/ die Fähre nach Konstanz?**
b **Wann geht/kommt/fährt sie in Konstanz an?**
c **Was kostet es einfach/hin und zurück?**

4 On the ferry you make friends with a German couple who invite you to join them for lunch. Look at the menu below and choose a fish starter, chicken as a main course and a light dessert.

Speisekarte
Restaurant Familie Bauer

Vorspeisen
Tagessuppe
Melone mit Kirschwasser
Heringssalat

Hauptgerichte
Jägerschnitzel mit Nudeln und Salat
Rumpsteak mit Pommes frites
Weißwurst mit Kartoffelsalat
Hähnchen mit Reis

Nachspeisen
frisches Obst
Nusstorte
Apfelkuchen mit Sahne

Now respond to the waiter's questions.

Ober	**Was möchten Sie als Vorspeise?**
You	....
Ober	**Und als Hauptgericht?**
You	....
Ober	**Möchten Sie eine Nachspeise?**
You	....

What does he say when he brings you your order?

a **Zahlen Sie bitte an der Kasse.**
b **Hat's geschmeckt?**
c **Guten Appetit!**

5 **2•76** After lunch you set off to do some shopping. You've asked a passer-by the way to a department store. Listen to the reply and note down the instructions.

....

6   2•77 You decide to buy something special for your sister's birthday next week. You see a display of smart leather handbags and go over to an assistant. Listen to the audio and take part in the conversation, noting down the two prices the assistant gives.

You'll need to know how to say:

- I'd like a handbag.
- How much do they cost?
- They're too expensive.
- That's nice, I'll take the bag.
- Can I pay by credit card?

7   2•78 Back in your hotel, you go down to the bar for a drink and get talking to a fellow guest, Silke Friedmann. Look at her side of the conversation below, fill in the questions you ask her, and then listen to check.

a   ....
     Ich wohne in Potsdam.
b   ....
     Ja, mein Mann heißt Martin.
c   ....
     Ja, einen Sohn, Dieter, und eine Tochter, Undine.
d   ....
     Sie ist fünfzehn.
e   ....
     Er ist achtzehn.
f   ....
     Ich bin Programmiererin und mein Mann ist Lehrer.
g   ....
     Ein Glas Weißwein, bitte.

Now order Silke's drink and a glass of red wine for yourself.

h   ....

8   In your hotel room you find some brochures and advertisements.
    Read them and see if you can answer the questions. There are some
    unfamiliar words – look them up in the glossary if you need to.

    a   Which restaurants are closed one day in the week and which days
        are they closed in each case?
    b   Where can you park for the **Rathauskeller**?
    c   Where exactly is the **Rathauskeller**?
    d   Where can you eat local specialities?
    e   Which restaurant stays open latest and on which days?
    f   Which two restaurants also offer accommodation?
    g   Next to the items on your shopping list below, write the name
        of the department you will need and the floor it is on in the
        Kaufcenter.

    leather gloves   ....
    local sausage   ....
    notepaper   ....
    box of chocolates   ....
    bottle of perfume   ....

    h   What else can you buy in the basement?
    i   Where is the earliest pick-up point for the Neuschwanstein
        excursion?
    j   What happens at 1.00 p.m.?
    k   How long is the coffee break?
    l   Where do you arrive at 8.40 p.m.?

Haus Vogtland
Restaurant und kleines Hotel

⌒⌒

Montag 09.00–14.00 und
17.00–22.00

Mittwoch–Samstag 9–22

Sonntag 9–20

Dienstag Ruhetag

10 Zimmer. Nur Apr.–Okt.
geöffnet

ZUM GOLDENEN LÖWEN
· ·

- **50 Zimmer mit Bad oder Dusche, Telefon, TV**
- **Geöffnet bis 23 Uhr**
- **Kinderspielplatz, Minigolf, Terrasse**
- **Parkplatz hinter dem Haus**

RESTAURANT RATHAUSKELLER
Lokale Spezialitäten – Internationale Gerichte

Ruhetag: Montag

Geöffnet: Dienstag–Freitag 12.00–22.00 Uhr

Samstag u. Sonntag 12.00–24.00 Uhr

*In der Altstadt gegenüber dem Dom
Parken auf dem Marktplatz*

KAUFCENTER	
2. Stock	Lederwaren Männermode Toiletten
1. Stock	Geschenke Parfum Frauenmode
Erdgeschoss	Schreibwaren Süßwaren
Untergeschoss	Lebensmittel Wein

Busfahrt nach Neuschwanstein

Abfahrt:	09.00	Hinter dem Rathaus
	09.10	Neben der Post
	09.20	Hotel Sonne

Kaffeepause: 11.00-11.30 in Königsstadt

Ankunft in Neuschwanstein: 13.00

Tour:	14.30
Abfahrt:	17.30

Ankunft:	20.30	Hotel Sonne
	20.40	Neben der Post
	20.50	Hinter dem Rathaus

Transcripts and answers

This section contains transcripts of all the conversations. Answers which consist of words and phrases from the conversations are given in bold type in the transcripts. Other answers are given separately, after each activity.

Unit 1

Pages 8 & 9 Saying hello and goodbye

2 *a* Guten Morgen, Frau Müller.
   b Tag, Rudi.
   c Guten Abend, Herr Braun.
   d Morgen, Frau Schmidt.
   e Guten Tag, Herr Scholz.
   a morning; b afternoon; c evening;
   d morning; e afternoon

3 First name: 1; Herr: 2; Frau: 2

5 *a* • Guten Abend, Herr Braun. Wie geht es Ihnen?
       ◆ Gut, danke, und Ihnen?
       ● Gut, danke.
   b ● Abend, Ulla. Wie geht's?
       ◆ Gut, danke.
   c ● Guten Abend, Rudi. Wie geht's?
       ◆ Gut, danke.
   The people in b and c know each other well.

7 ● **Auf Wiedersehen!**
   ◆ **Tschüs**, Maria.
   ● **Gute Nacht**, Rudi.
   ◆ **Wiedersehen**, Frau Engel.

8 *a* Tschüs, Helga, gute Nacht.
   b Guten Abend, Frau Onken. Wie geht es Ihnen?
   c Guten Abend, Herr Kunz.
   d Wiedersehen, Hannelore.
   e Auf Wiedersehen, Herr Brammerts.
   The people in a, d and e are leaving.

9 Morgen, Barbara.
   Guten Abend, Herr Scholz.
   Guten Morgen, Frau Hoffmann.
   Tag, Manfred.
   Guten Abend, Rudi.
   Barbara: Wie geht's?/Herr Scholz: Wie geht es Ihnen?
   Manfred: Tschüs./Rudi: (Auf) Wiedersehen.

Pages 10 & 11 Introducing yourself and socializing

2 ● Guten **Tag**. Mein Name ist **Müller**, **Heinrich Müller**.
   ◆ Guten Tag, Herr Müller.
   ● Guten **Abend**, ich heiße **Blum**, **Anna**.
   ◆ Ja, guten Abend, Frau Blum.
   ● Guten **Abend**, ich heiße **Barbara Goldmann**.
   ◆ Guten Abend, Frau Goldmann.
   ● Guten **Tag**. Mein Name ist **Brammerts**.
   ◆ Guten Tag, Herr Brammerts.

3 ● Guten Tag. Wie heißen Sie, bitte?
   ◆ **Ich heiße** Altmann, Georg Altmann.

6 ● Wie heißen **Sie**?
   ◆ Ich **heiße** Georg Altmann. Und Sie?
   ● Mein **Name** ist Schwarz, Maria Schwarz.
   ◆ Wie bitte?
   ● Maria Schwarz.
   ◆ **Freut mich**, Frau Schwarz.

8 *a* ● Tag, **Jutta**. Wie geht's?
       ◆ Gut, danke, **Liesl**.
   b ● Guten Tag. Ich heiße **Dieter** Scholz.
       ◆ Guten Tag, Herr Scholz.
   c ● Wie heißen Sie?
       ◆ Ich heiße **Manfred**.
   d ● Und mein Name ist **Kerstin**. Wie heißen Sie?
       ◆ Mein Name ist **Inge**.

Page 12 Put it all together

1 *a* Goodbye; *b* What's your name?;
c Bye; *d* Good afternoon; *e* Pardon;
f Good night; *g* Pleased to meet you;
h How are you?

2 *a* Guten Morgen; *b* Guten Abend;
c Guten Tag; *d* Tschüs

3 *c, b, e, a, d*

Page 13 Now you're talking!

1 ● **Guten Tag.**
   ◆ Guten Tag. Wie geht es Ihnen?
   ● **Gut, danke. Und Ihnen?**
   ◆ Gut, danke.

2 ● **Guten Tag! Ich heiße (your
   name).**
   ◆ Freut mich. Ich heiße Schneider,
   Anna Schneider.
   ● **Wie bitte?**
   ◆ Frau Schneider, Anna Schneider.
   ● **Es freut mich, Frau Schneider.**

3 ● **Guten Tag. Wie heißen Sie,
   bitte?**
   ◆ Mein Name ist Offenbach.
   ● **Es freut mich, Herr Offenbach.
   Ich heiße (your name).**

4 ● **Auf Wiedersehen, Frau
   Schneider. Auf Wiedersehen,
   Herr Offenbach.**

5 ● **Auf Wiedersehen, Frau Meyer,
   gute Nacht.**

Page 14 Quiz

1 When saying goodbye to someone
you know well; *2* Ich heiße …;
3 Mein Name ist …; *4* When
you haven't heard/understood
something; *5* Es freut mich;
6 Gute Nacht; *7* Wie geht's?
8 Morning

Unit 2

Pages 16 & 17 Saying where you're
from and where your home town is

2 ● Woher kommen Sie?
   ◆ **Ich bin Engländer.**
   ● Und Sie? Woher kommen Sie?
   ◆ Ich komme aus Irland.
   ● Gut. Und Sie? Kommen Sie aus
   England?
   ◆ Nein, ich komme aus Wales. Ich
   bin Waliserin.
   ● Sind Sie Engländer?
   ◆ **Ja, ich bin Engländer.**
   Two of the people are English.

3/4
   ● Ich bin **Spanier.**
   ◆ Ich komme aus Italien. Ich bin
   Italienerin.
   ● Ich bin **Schottin.**
   ◆ Ich bin **Kanadierin.**
   ● Ich komme aus Australien. Ich bin
   Australier.
   ◆ Ich bin **Irin.**
   ● Ich bin **Amerikaner.**
   ◆ Ich bin **Österreicherin.**
   There are 3 men and 5 women.
   Spanish, Italian, Scottish, Canadian,
   Australian, Irish, American, Austrian

6 ● Ich heiße Peter Davies. Ich wohne
   in **Cardiff** in **Wales.**
   ◆ Mein Name ist Irene Fischer.
   Ich wohne in **Hamburg** in
   Deutschland.
   ● Ich komme aus **Perth** in
   Schottland. Mein Name ist John
   McPhee.
   ◆ Mein Name ist Maeve Sullivan. Ich
   wohne in **Waterford** in **Irland.**

7 ● Wo **wohnen** Sie, Frau Schwarz?
   ◆ Ich **wohne** in Wien in Österreich.
   ● **Wo** wohnen Sie?
   ◆ Ich wohne **in** Bozen in **Italien.**
   ● Und wo wohnen **Sie?** Sind Sie
   Italiener?
   ◆ Nein, ich bin Spanier. **Ich** wohne in
   Madrid.

Page 18 Saying what you do

2 policewoman = Polizistin; student = Student; computer programmer = Programmierer; 3 refer to women.

3 ● Frau Sullivan, was sind Sie?
  ◆ Ich bin **Lehrerin**.
  ● Und was sind Sie, Frau Fischer?
  ◆ Ich bin **Hausfrau**.
  ● Herr Smith, was sind Sie?
  ◆ Ich bin **Sekretär**.
  ● Und was sind Sie, Frau Pastena?
  ◆ Ich bin **Polizistin**.
  ● Und Sie, Herr McPhee?
  ◆ Ich bin **Programmierer**.
  ● Und was sind Sie, Herr Davies?
  ◆ Ich bin **Student**.
  teacher, housewife, secretary, policewoman, computer programmer, student

Page 19 Using the numbers from 0 to 10

2 **drei**; neun; vier; **sechs**; **acht**; fünf

3 ● Was ist Ihre Telefonnummer, Frau Fischer?
  ◆ **Vier, sechs, zwo, fünf, drei, acht**.
  ● Was ist Ihre Telefonnummer, Herr Smith?
  ◆ **Acht, zwo, drei, neun, fünf, eins**.
  ● Und Ihre Telefonnummer, Herr Davies?
  ◆ **Sechs, sieben, eins, fünf, zwo, sechs**.
  Irene: 462538; Mark: 823951; Peter: 671526

4 ● Sieben, null, vier, fünf, sechs, acht.
  ◆ Fünf, neun, eins, sechs, sieben, vier.
  ● Eins, zwo, fünf, drei, sechs, sieben, drei, zwo.
  ◆ Acht, fünf, drei, eins, neun, sieben.

Page 20 Put it all together

1 *a* Ich bin Kanadier; *b* Aus Amerika; *c* Nein, ich komme aus Irland; *d* Ich wohne in Stirling; *e* Ich bin Hausfrau; *f* 01982 46723

2 Helen Brownsmith: American; Washington; teacher
Georg Müller: Austrian; Salzburg; computer programmer
Andrew Hyde: Scottish; Glasgow; policeman

3 Ich heiße Dieter Hoffmann. Ich bin Österreicher und ich wohne in Wien. Ich bin arbeitslos.
Ich heiße Juanita Pueblos. Ich bin Spanierin. Ich wohne in Madrid und ich bin Studentin.

Page 21 Now you're talking!

1 ● Sind Sie Ausländerin?
  ◆ **Ja, ich bin Amerikanerin**.
  ● Wo wohnen Sie?
  ◆ **Ich wohne in Washington**.
  ● Was sind Sie?
  ◆ **Ich bin Lehrerin**.

2 ● Herr Jones, sind Sie Engländer?
  ◆ **Nein, ich bin Waliser**.
  ● Wo wohnen Sie in Wales?
  ◆ **Ich wohne in Cardiff**.
  ● Was sind Sie?
  ◆ **Ich bin Mechaniker**.
  ● Und was ist Ihre Telefonnummer?
  ◆ **Null, eins, sechs, vier, drei, neun, sieben, fünf, acht**.

3 ● **Wie heißen Sie?**
  ◆ Ich heiße Ulrike Dietrich.
  ● **Wo wohnen Sie?**
  ◆ Ich wohne in Kiel in Deutschland.
  ● **Was sind Sie?**
  ◆ Ich bin Stewardess bei Lufthansa.

Page 22 Quiz

1 Ich bin Amerikanerin; *2* Wohnen Sie in Leipzig? *3* Ich komme aus Chester; *4* Nein, ich bin (your nationality); *5* Ich bin Studentin; *6* Austria; *7* vier, sieben; *8* Schottin

Unit 3

Pages 24 & 25 Ordering a drink in a bar and in a café

2 ● Ich möchte **ein Glas Rotwein**, bitte.
  ◆ **Ein Mineralwasser**, bitte.
  ● **Ein Bier**, bitte.
  ◆ Ich möchte **eine Cola**.

3 ● Guten Tag! Bitte schön?
  ◆ Ein **Mineralwasser**, bitte.
  ● Ein **Bier**, bitte.
  ◆ Und Sie?
  ● Eine **Cola**, bitte.
  ◆ Ein **Glas Rotwein** … nein, ein **Glas Weißwein**, bitte.
  Helen: mineral water; Georg: beer; Irene: coke; Peter: glass of white wine

5 ● Eine Tasse Tee mit Milch, bitte.
  ◆ Ein Kännchen Kaffee mit Sahne, bitte.
  ● Ein Kännchen Tee mit Milch, bitte.
  ◆ Eine Tasse Kaffee ohne Milch, bitte.
  ● Eine Schokolade, bitte.
  ◆ Ein Kännchen Tee, bitte.

6 Ein Kännchen Tee mit Milch, bitte; Ein Kännchen Kaffee, bitte; Eine Tasse Tee ohne Milch, bitte; Zwei Tassen Kaffee mit Sahne, bitte.

Pages 26 & 27 Offering someone a drink and accepting or refusing

2 ● Maria, was **möchten** Sie?
  ◆ Oh, ein **Glas** Wein, bitte.
  ● Ein Glas **Weißwein**?
  ◆ Nein, **Rotwein**, **bitte**.
  ● Und **für** Sie, Franz? **Noch** einen Kaffee?

3 Möchten Sie einen Kaffee?; Möchten Sie ein Glas Bier?; Möchten Sie eine Tasse Tee mit Milch?; Möchten Sie noch einen Kaffee?; Möchten Sie eine Cola?

5 ● Barbara, möchten Sie ein Bier?
  ◆ Gern.
  ● Manfred, möchten Sie ein Glas Wein?

  ◆ Nein, danke.
  ● Irene, was möchten Sie?
  ◆ Für mich nichts, danke.
  ● Angelika, möchten Sie einen Kaffee?
  ◆ Ja, danke.
  ● Franz, möchten Sie ein Glas Rotwein?
  ◆ Ja, gern … danke schön … Prost!
  Barbara, Angelika and Franz accept.

6 *c* is Georg's bill.

7 Prost!; Danke schön.

Page 28 Put it all together

1 *Irene* Drei Glas Weißwein und ein Bier, bitte.
  Mann Drei Bier, eine Cola und ein Mineralwasser, bitte.

2 1 *b*; 2 *c*; 3 *a*; 4 *c*.

3 *Jutta* Ich **möchte einen** Kaffee, bitte. Und für **Sie**, Liesl?
  Liesl Für **mich** ein Bier.
  Manfred Für mich **nichts**, **danke**.
  Jutta Gut. Ein Bier und einen Kaffee, **bitte**.
  Jutta **Nein**, danke.

Page 29 Now you're talking!

1 ● Möchten Sie einen Kaffee?
  ◆ **Ja, gern.**
  ● Mit oder ohne Sahne?
  ◆ **Mit Sahne, bitte.**
  ● **Was möchten Sie, Franz?**
  ◆ Ein Mineralwasser, bitte.
  ● **Irene, möchten Sie noch einen Kaffee?**
  ◆ Ja, danke.
  ● **Ein Mineralwasser, eine Tasse Kaffee und ein Kännchen Tee, bitte.**

2 ● Bitte schön?
  ◆ **Eine Tasse Tee mit Milch und zwei Kännchen Kaffee, bitte.**
  ● Bitte schön?
  ◆ **Ein Glas Weißwein, zwei Glas Cola und vier Bier, bitte.**

3 ● Bitte schön?
  ◆ **Möchten Sie ein Bier?**
  ● Ja, gern.
  ◆ **Dieter, was möchten Sie?**
  ● Für mich ein Glas Bier.
  ◆ **Und Sie, Kerstin?**
  ● Für mich ein Glas Rotwein.
  ◆ **Zwei Glas Bier, ein Glas Rotwein und ein Glas Weißwein, bitte.**
  ● Sonst noch etwas?
  ◆ **Nein, danke.**
  ● **Danke ... Prost!**

Page 30 Quiz

1 white; *2* Rotwein; *3* accepting; *4* three more beers; *5* do you want anything else? *6* Bier, Wein; *7* Kaffee; *8* ein Kännchen

Unit 4

Page 32 Introducing someone

2 *a* ● Darf ich **vorstellen**? Das **ist** mein Mann, Karl Fischer.
    ◆ Freut mich. Mein Name ist Joachim Schneider.
  b ● **Darf** ich vorstellen? Das **sind** meine Freunde, Bob und Joan Butler.
    ◆ Es freut mich, Herr Butler, Frau Butler.
    ● **Ebenfalls.**

3 *Liesl* Darf ich vorstellen? **Das ist mein Mann.**

 Hans **Darf ich vorstellen? Das ist meine Frau.**

Page 33 Talking about family

2 ● Sind Sie verheiratet, Brigitte?
  ◆ **Ja, ich bin verheiratet.**
  ● Sind Sie verheiratet, Herr Koch?
  ◆ Nein, ich bin nicht verheiratet.
  ● Und Sie, Frau Schwarz, sind Sie verheiratet?
  ◆ Nein, ich bin nicht verheiratet.
  Brigitte is married.

4 ● Frau Fischer, sind Sie verheiratet?
  ◆ Ja, ich bin verheiratet.
  ● Haben Sie Kinder?
  ◆ Ja, ich habe einen Sohn.
  ● Und Sie, Herr Schneider, sind Sie verheiratet?
  ◆ Ja, und ich habe eine Tochter und einen Sohn.
  ● Und Sie, Herr Müller?
  ◆ Ich bin nicht verheiratet und ich habe keine Kinder.
  Irene: verheiratet; 1 Sohn
  Joachim: verheiratet; 1 Tochter, 1 Sohn
  Georg: nicht verheiratet; –

Page 34 Asking and giving someone's age

3 ● Mein Sohn **Fritz ist siebzehn** und meine Tochter **Maria ist zwölf.**
  ◆ Ich habe zwei Töchter: **Liesl ist fünfzehn** und **Jutta ist dreizehn.**
  Fritz: 17; Maria: 12; Liesl: 15; Jutta: 13

4 Mein Sohn Manfred **ist neunzehn.** Meine **Tochter Angelika ist sechzehn.**
  Mein Sohn Daniel ist elf.

Page 35 Using the numbers up to 100

2 **sechs**undzwanzig, siebenund**zwanzig**, **acht**undzwanzig, neun**undzwanzig**

4 **drei**undvierzig; **fünf**undvierzig; sechsund**vierzig**; siebenun**und**vierzig; **neunundvierzig**

5 *a* Meine Frau ist **zweiunddreißig.**
  b Mein Sohn Michael ist **fünfzehn.**
  c Mein Mann ist **vierundsechzig.**
  d Meine Tochter ist **siebzehn.**
  e Meine Frau ist **vierundneunzig.**
  a 32; b 15; c 64; d 17; e 94

Page 36 Put it all together

1 Darf ich vorstellen? Mein Name ist Jack Bradshaw. Ich bin verheiratet und habe einen Sohn und eine Tochter. Ich bin achtundvierzig Jahre alt, meine Frau Mary ist

siebenundvierzig. Mein Sohn Frank ist sechsundzwanzig und meine Tochter Julia ist vierundzwanzig.

2 *d, b, f, e, a, c*

3 Familie Schröder: 48; Familie Lindemann: 49; Familie Martens: 51; Familie Förster: 52

Page 37 Now you're talking!

1 ● Wie heißen Sie?
  ◆ **Ich heiße Robert Blythe.**
  ● Sind Sie verheiratet?
  ◆ **Ja, ich bin verheiratet. Meine Frau heißt Clare.**
  ● Und haben Sie Kinder?
  ◆ **Ja, ich habe eine Tochter, Jenny.**
  ● Haben Sie einen Sohn?
  ◆ **Nein.**
  ● Wie alt ist Jenny?
  ◆ **Sie ist elf.**

2 ● Darf ich vorstellen? Das sind meine Freunde, Stephanie und Georg Krumm … Herr Blythe.
  ◆ Freut mich, Herr Blythe.
  ● **Ebenfalls, Frau Krumm.**
  ◆ **Das ist meine Frau, Clare … Herr und Frau Krumm.**
  ● Freut mich, Frau Blythe.

3 ● **Haben Sie Kinder?**
  ◆ Ja, ich habe einen Sohn.
  ● **Wie alt ist er?**
  ◆ Er ist vierzehn.

Page 38 Quiz

1 Das ist mein Mann; *2* Ebenfalls; *3* They haven't any children; *4* Ich bin … Jahre alt; *5* 18; *6* sie; *7* married; *8* Ich habe drei Söhne.

Kontrollpunkt 1
Pages 39–42

1 *a* Ja, einen Sohn; *b* Prost!; *c* Nein, danke; *d* Guten Abend!; *e* Sind Sie verheiratet?; *f* Gute Nacht; *g* Aus England.

2 ● Guten Abend. Ich heiße Detlev. Wie heißen Sie?
  ◆ Mein Name ist Sylvia. Ich bin Italienerin. Woher kommen Sie?
  ● Ich wohne in Wunstdorf in Deutschland. Ich bin Mechaniker.
  ◆ Ich bin Sekretärin.
  ● Sind Sie verheiratet?
  ◆ Nein. Und Sie?
  ● Ja, ich bin verheiratet.
  ◆ Haben Sie Kinder?
  ● Ja, zwei Töchter. Annaliese ist einundzwanzig und Lore ist achtzehn.
  Detlev: German; mechanic; married, 2 daughters
  Sylvia: Italian; secretary; unmarried

3 ● Wie heißen Sie, bitte?
  ◆ Mein Name ist Miller, Margaret Miller.
  ● Sind Sie Engländerin, Frau Miller?
  ◆ Nein, ich komme **aus Australien.**
  ● Und was sind Sie?
  ◆ Ich bin **Lehrerin.**
  ● Und wie alt sind Sie, bitte?
  ◆ Ich bin **fünfunddreißig.**
  ● Sind Sie verheiratet, Frau Miller?
  ◆ Ja, und ich habe **eine Tochter.**
  ● Und wie heißen Sie?
  ◆ Ich heiße Steven Carter.
  ● Woher kommen Sie, Herr Carter?
  ◆ Ich komme **aus Hull in England.**
  ● Und was sind Sie?
  ◆ Ich bin **Polizist.**
  ● Sind Sie verheiratet, Herr Carter?
  ◆ Ja.
  ● Und haben Sie Kinder?
  ◆ Nein, ich habe **keine Kinder.**
  ● Und wie alt sind Sie?
  ◆ **Zweiunddreißig.**
  Errors: Kanadierin ➔ Australierin; Polizistin ➔ Lehrerin; einen Sohn ➔ eine Tochter; Lehrer ➔ Polizist; 42 ➔ 32

4 ● Brigitte, was möchten Sie?
  ◆ Oh, **ein Glas Weißwein**, bitte.
  ● Gut. Ach, Frau Fischer und Herr Müller! Guten Abend!
  ◆ Guten Abend!
  ● Was möchten Sie?
  ◆ Für mich **Tee**, bitte.

- Mit Milch?
- Ja, mit Milch.
- Und für Sie, Herr Müller?
- **Ein Bier**, bitte.
- Ein Glas Weißwein, ein Kännchen Tee mit Milch und zwei Bier, bitte.
  Brigitte: glass of white wine; Irene: pot of tea with milk; Georg: beer; Joachim: beer

5 *a* einundsiebzig, zwölf, neunundachtzig, fünfundvierzig, vierundfünfzig
  b Meine Telefonnummer ist eins, sieben, acht, zwo, fünf, drei. *(178253)*

6 *a* Wie heißen Sie? *b* Wie alt sind Sie? *c* Sind Sie verheiratet? *d* Was sind Sie?

7 ● Bitte schön?
  ◆ Eine Tasse Kaffee, eine Limonade, ein Bier, ein Glas Rotwein und ein Glas Weißwein, bitte.

8 Missing words: **heiße**; Deut**schland**; **alt**; Programm**ierer**; **Student**in; verhe**iratet**; **kommt**; **arbeits**los; Lehr**erin**
  a Susi is a student and Jochen is unemployed; *b* His father is a computer programmer and his mother is a secretary; *c* 14; *d* Italian

9 *a* GUTEN MORGEN; *b* AUF WIEDERSEHEN; *c* TSCHÜS; *d* MEIN NAME IST; *e* FREUT MICH; *f* DANKE; *g* ICH BIN; *h* GUTEN ABEND; *i* WIE GEHT ES IHNEN

Unit 5

Pages 44 & 45 Enquiring about places in town and understanding where they are

2 ● Entschuldigen Sie, wo ist **die Post**?
  ● Wo ist **der Bahnhof**, bitte? Ist das weit von hier?
  ◆ Wo ist **das Rathaus**, bitte?
  ● Ist das **der Marktplatz**?
  ◆ Entschuldigen Sie, ist das **die Bank**?

3 *a* Entschuldigen Sie, **wo ist** der Bahnhof, bitte?
  b Wo ist der Dom? Ist das **weit** von hier?
  c Wo ist **die Bank**, bitte?
  d **Entschuldigen** Sie, ist das das Verkehrs**amt**?
  e Ist das Einkaufszentrum weit **von hier**?

5 *a* ● Wo ist der Bahnhof, Brigitte?
      ◆ Wir sind hier … und der Bahnhof ist da drüben.
  b ● Ach ja, und da ist die Post auch links.
  c ● Gut. Und wo ist das Einkaufszentrum?
      ◆ Das Einkaufszentrum? Rechts.
  d ● Danke, und wo ist die Apotheke?
      ◆ Die Apotheke ist geradeaus.
      ● Ist das weit von hier?
      ◆ Nein, vielleicht zehn Minuten zu Fuß.
  e ● Und der Dom ist hier rechts.
  a Bahnhof, O; b Post, L; c Einkaufszentrum, R; d Apotheke, S; e Dom, R

6 *1* der Bahnhof; *2* das Verkehrsamt; *3* das Rathaus; *4* der Dom; *5* die Apotheke

7 Wo ist der Bahnhof?; Wo ist das Verkehrsamt?; Wo ist der Dom?

Page 46 Following simple directions

2 *a* ● Der Dom? Gehen Sie geradeaus und dann **links**.
  b ● Wo ist das Verkehrsamt, bitte?
      ◆ Da drüben, neben der Bank.
  c ● Wo ist der Bahnhof, bitte?
      ◆ Gehen Sie hier links.
  d ● Wo ist das Einkaufszentrum, bitte?
      ◆ Gehen Sie rechts um die Ecke.
  e ● Ist der Dom gegenüber der Bank?
      ◆ Nein, **gegenüber dem Rathaus**.
  f ● Wo ist die Apotheke, bitte?
      ◆ Nehmen Sie die zweite Straße **links** und die Apotheke ist neben der Post.

3 *a* Das Museum ist neben **dem** Bahnhof.

b Der Parkplatz ist nicht weit von **der** Bank.

c Die Post ist gegenüber **dem** Einkaufszentrum.

d Der Dom ist neben **dem** Marktplatz.

Page 47 Asking for help with understanding

2 • Entschuldigen Sie, ich bin fremd hier. Wo ist das Rathaus?

♦ Gehen Sie hier geradeaus.

• Entschuldigen Sie, wo ist der Dom?

♦ Gehen Sie hier links, nehmen Sie die zweite Straße rechts, dann geradeaus …

• Bitte wiederholen Sie, ich verstehe nicht.

♦ Entschuldigen Sie, wo ist das Verkehrsamt?

• Hier rechts, dann geradeaus, vielleicht fünf Minuten, dann links …

♦ Sprechen Sie langsamer, bitte.

• Entschuldigen Sie, ich bin fremd hier. Wo ist die Post?

♦ Um die Ecke, gegenüber dem Einkaufszentrum.

• Ach, das Einkaufszentrum ist auch um die Ecke?

Irene: town hall; stranger here
Anna: cathedral; doesn't understand, please repeat
Maria: tourist office; too fast, speak more slowly
Jutta: post office; stranger here

3 *a* Sprechen Sie langsamer, bitte (Ich verstehe nicht); *b* Ich bin fremd hier; *c* Bitte wiederholen Sie (Ich verstehe nicht); *d* Ich verstehe nicht.

Page 48 Put it all together

1 Wo ist … *a* die Bank? *b* die Apotheke? *c* das Rathaus? *d* der Bahnhof? *e* der Dom? *f* das Verkehrsamt?

2 *a* das Einkaufszentrum; *b* das Verkehrsamt; *c* die Apotheke; *d* der Marktplatz

3 *a* Gehen Sie geradeaus. Das Museum ist da rechts.

b (Gehen Sie geradeaus,) nehmen Sie die zweite Straße links. Die Bank ist da rechts.

Page 49 Now you're talking!

1 • **Guten Morgen. Wo ist der Dom, bitte?**

♦ Der Dom? Der Dom ist neben dem Rathaus.

• **Ist das weit?**

♦ Nein, zehn Minuten zu Fuß.

• **Und wo ist die Bank?**

♦ Gegenüber dem Rathaus.

• **Danke. Auf Wiedersehen.**

2 • **Entschuldigen Sie, wo ist das Einkaufszentrum?**

♦ Das ist nicht weit – geradeaus, die zweite Straße rechts und da ist es.

• **Bitte wiederholen Sie.**

♦ Das ist nicht weit – immer geradeaus, die zweite Straße rechts und da ist es.

• **Ich verstehe nicht. Sprechen Sie langsamer, bitte.**

3 • **Entschuldigen Sie, ich bin fremd hier.**

♦ Ja?

• **Wo ist das Verkehrsamt, bitte?**

♦ Gehen Sie rechts um die Ecke.

• **Danke. Auf Wiedersehen.**

4 • **Gehen Sie geradeaus. Nehmen Sie die erste Straße rechts. Der Dom ist links neben dem Rathaus.**

Page 50 Quiz

1 The shopping centre is over there; *2* Wo ist die Apotheke?; *3* Ich verstehe nicht; *4* Go straight ahead; *5* Take the second road on the left; *6* When someone speaks too fast; *7* neben; *8* Verkehrsbüro

Unit 6

Pages 52 & 53 Asking for what you want and understanding the assistant

2 a Was kosten die Orangen, bitte?
  b Haben Sie Bananen?
  c Eine Ananas und drei Orangen, bitte.
  a oranges; b bananas; c a pineapple and three oranges

3 ● Bitte schön?
  ◆ Was **kosten** die Bananen?
  ● Vier Bananen kosten einen Euro fünfzig.
  ◆ Und **haben** Sie Orangen?
  ● Ja, hier. Eine Orange **kostet** dreißig Cent.
  ◆ Ich möchte sechs.
  ● Sonst noch etwas?
  ◆ Ja, was **kostet** eine Ananas?
  ● Zwei Euro fünfzig.
  ◆ Gut. Vier Bananen, sechs Orangen und eine Ananas, bitte.

5 a ● Guten Tag. **Kann ich Ihnen helfen?**
    ◆ Ja, ich möchte sechs Tomaten, bitte.
    ● Sechs Tomaten kosten einen Euro vierzig. Sonst noch etwas?
    ◆ Ja, und die Trauben.
    ● **Die hier?** Gut. Sie kosten drei Euro zwanzig **das Kilo.**
    ◆ Danke.
  b ● Guten Tag.
    ◆ Guten Tag. Ich möchte Brötchen, bitte. Was kosten sie?
    ● Dreißig Cent **das Stück.**
    ◆ Ich möchte zehn, bitte.

6 € 1,40; € 3,20; Ct. 30; total € 4,90

Page 54 Buying the quantity you want

2 a zweihundertfünfzig Gramm Trauben (*250 g*); b ein halber Liter Milch (*½ l*); c ein Liter Rotwein (*1 l*); d und ein halbes Kilo Tomaten (*½ kg*).

3 ● Guten Morgen. Ich möchte **eine Flasche Orangensaft**, bitte.
  ◆ Kann ich Ihnen helfen?
  ● Ja, **eine Dose Tomaten**, bitte.
  ◆ Ich möchte **ein Päckchen Kekse.**
  ● Ich möchte **eine Packung Apfelsaft**, bitte.

4 Eine **Flasche** Orangensaft, ein halbes Kilo **Bananen**, ein Liter **Mineralwasser**, ein **Päckchen** Kaffee, sechs **Brötchen**, eine **Dose** Cola, eine Packung **Milch** und **hundert Gramm** Tee.

Page 55 Dealing with money

2 ● Entschuldigen Sie. Wo kann ich **Geld wechseln**?
  ◆ In der Bank um die Ecke.
  ● Das macht € 49, bitte.
  ◆ Kann ich Ihnen helfen?
  ● Ja, ich möchte diesen **Reisescheck einlösen**.
  ◆ Kann ich **mit Kreditkarte bezahlen**?
  ● Mit Kreditkarte? Ja, kein Problem!
  Manfred: change money; Georg: cash a traveller's cheque; Maria: pay by credit card

3 a wechseln; b einlösen; c einlösen

Page 56 Put it all together

1 Trauben: 250 g; Apfelsaft: Flasche/ 1 Liter; Kekse: Päckchen; Wein: Flasche/1 Liter; Cola: Flasche/Dose

2 eine Flasche Orangensaft; ein Liter Rotwein; ein halbes Kilo Tomaten; vier Bananen; eine Dose Tomaten; ein Päckchen Kekse; sechs Brötchen

3 a Was kosten die Orangen?
  b Ich möchte diesen Reisescheck einlösen.
  c Wo kann ich Geld wechseln?
  d Kann ich Ihnen helfen?
  e Was kostet eine Ananas?
  f Kann ich mit Kreditkarte bezahlen?

Page 57 Now you're talking!

1 ● Tag. Kann ich Ihnen helfen?
  ◆ **Guten Tag. Zweihundertfünfzig Gramm Trauben und ein Kilo Bananen, bitte.**
  ● Sonst noch etwas?
  ◆ **Ich möchte ein halbes Kilo Tomaten.**
  ● Gut. Und sonst noch etwas?
  ◆ **Nein, das ist alles. Danke schön.**

2 ● **Ich möchte sechs Brötchen, bitte.**
  ◆ Sonst noch etwas?
  ● **Was kostet ein Päckchen Kekse?**
  ◆ Einen Euro fünfzig das Päckchen.
  ● **Ich möchte ein Päckchen und eine Flasche Rotwein.**
  ◆ Sonst noch etwas?
  ● **Ja, ich möchte einen Liter Apfelsaft.**
  ◆ Gut. Zehn Euro achtzig, bitte.

3 ● **Guten Tag. Ich möchte Geld wechseln.**
  ◆ Ja, gut … das sind dann zweihundertfünfzehn Euro.
  ● **Danke. Auf Wiedersehen.**

Page 58 Quiz

1a Was kosten? *b* Was kostet? *c* Was kostet?; 2 Haben Sie Tomaten?; 3 100; 4 Ein Tomatenbrötchen, bitte; 5 einlösen; 6 ¼ litre; 7 10 oranges; 8 Packung

Unit 7

Pages 60 & 61 Finding the right department in a department store

2 *a* die Schreibwarenabteilung; *b* die Haushaltswarenabteilung; *c* die Lederwarenabteilung

3 ● Entschuldigen Sie. Wo finde ich die Sportabteilung?
  ◆ Die Sportabteilung ist im zweiten Stock.
  ● Wo finde ich Süßwaren?
  ◆ Im dritten Stock.
  ● Wo finde ich Lederwaren, bitte?
  ◆ Die Lederwarenabteilung ist im ersten Stock.

sports department – second floor; leather goods – first floor; confectionery – third floor

5 *a* Der Parkplatz ist im Erdgeschoss.
  b Die Toiletten sind auch im Erdgeschoss.
  c Das Restaurant? Das ist im dritten Stock.
  a richtig; b falsch; c falsch

6 *a* ● Entschuldigen Sie. Wo **sind** die Toiletten?
    ◆ Die Toiletten? Sie sind **im Erdgeschoss**, neben dem Parkplatz.
  b ● Wo **ist** das Restaurant?
    ◆ Gegenüber der Bank **im dritten Stock**.
  c ● Wo finde ich Geschenke?
    ◆ Die Geschenkabteilung ist **im Untergeschoss**.

Page 62 Getting just what you want

2 *a* ● Ich möchte **Pralinen**, bitte.
    ◆ Die Pralinen hier?
    ● Ja, die sind **schön**.
  b ● Was kostet eine **Flasche Wein?**
    ◆ Diese Flasche kostet vierunddreißig Euro.
    ● Oh, das ist **zu teuer**.
  c ● Ich suche **eine Tasche**, aber die Tasche hier ist **zu groß**.
    ◆ Möchten Sie vielleicht die Tasche da?
  a chocolates, nice; b bottle of wine, too expensive; c handbag, too big

3 ● Ich suche ein T-Shirt.
  ◆ Das T-Shirt hier ist schön.
  ● Ja, aber das ist zu klein.
  ◆ Ich suche eine Flasche Rotwein. Was kostet diese Flasche?
  ● Zwei Euro sechzig.
  ◆ Ja, gut.
  ● Was kostet die Tasche, bitte?
  ◆ Fünf Euro fünfundvierzig.
  ● Oh, das ist nicht teuer.
  ◆ Haben Sie Pralinen?
  ● Ja, die hier kosten vierzehn Euro fünfzig.
  ◆ Oh, die sind zu teuer!
  Kerstin may buy the wine and the bag.

4 Das ist zu groß; Ich nehme eine
Flasche Wein; Ich suche eine Tasche.

Page 63 Understanding opening times

2 Store *b* is open Monday–Friday.

3 *a* Wir sind von neun bis sechs
geöffnet. Dienstag ist Ruhetag.
b Wir sind von acht bis zwölf und
von zwei bis sechs geöffnet. Wir
sind montags geschlossen.
c Wir sind von neun bis eins und
von zwei bis sieben geöffnet.
Donnerstag ist Ruhetag.
a 9 a.m.–6 p.m., closed Tuesdays;
b 8–12 a.m. and 2–6 p.m., closed
Mondays; *c* 9 a.m. –1 p.m. & 2–7 p.m.,
closed Thursdays

Page 64 Put it all together

1 *a* Tuesday rest day; *b* toilets in the
basement; *c* open from 8 to 12 and
from 2 to 7; *d* restaurant closed until
Thursday

2 *b*, *d*, *e*, *c*, *a*

3 *a* expensive; *b* big; *c* nice; *d* small

4 *a* Lederwarenabteilung;
b Süßwarenabteilung;
c Lebensmittelabteilung;
d Haushaltswarenabteilung

Page 65 Now you're talking!

1 ● **Entschuldigen Sie. Wo sind die
Toiletten?**
◆ Die Toiletten sind im zweiten
Stock.
● **Danke. Wo finde ich die
Sportabteilung?**
◆ Im Erdgeschoss.
● **Ist das neben der
Lebensmittelabteilung?**
◆ Ja, neben der
Lebensmittelabteilung.

2 ● **Ich suche Geschenke.**
◆ Vielleicht Pralinen?
● **Die sind zu teuer.**
◆ Eine Tasche? Oder eine Flasche

Wein?
● **Was kostet eine Tasche?**
◆ Fünfundzwanzig Euro.
● **Gut. Ich nehme eine Tasche.**

3 ● **Wann sind Sie geöffnet?**
◆ Wir sind von neun bis sechs
geöffnet. Montag ist Ruhetag.
● **Wo ist der Parkplatz?**
◆ Im Untergeschoss, neben der
Haushaltswarenabteilung.
● **Danke. Auf Wiedersehen.**

Page 66 Quiz

1 Mittwoch; *2* geöffnet;
3 im Restaurant and in der
Lebensmittelabteilung (food
department); *4* We're closed on
Wednesdays; *5* Samstag, Sonnabend;
6 Untergeschoss; *7* the T-shirt; *8* in
der Schreibwarenabteilung

Kontrollpunkt 2
Pages 67–70

1 *a* the chemist's; *b* the station;
c first road on the right; *d* the tourist
information office; *e* straight ahead;
f on the third floor; *g* the restaurant;
h opposite; *i* left; *j* in the stationery
department

2 *1* COLA; *2* KAFFEE; *3* KEKSE;
4 ANANAS; *5* ORANGEN;
6 APFELSAFT; *7* FLASCHE;
8 BANANEN; *9* DOSE; *10* WEIN;
11 TOMATEN; *12* TRAUBEN

3 **eine** Ananas; **sechs Dosen** Cola;
ein halbes Kilo Trauben;
ein Päckchen Kaffee; **fünf** Orangen;
eine Flasche Weißwein

4 *a* ● Was kostet der Wein?
◆ Sieben Euro.
b ● Die Tasche kostet
siebenundsechzig Euro fünfzig?
Oh, das ist teuer!
c ● Das kostet **zwei Euro dreißig**. Gut!
d ● Was kosten die Pralinen?
◆ Vierzehn Euro zwanzig.

e ● Die kosten **vierzig Euro**.
f ● Was kostet das T-Shirt?
  ◆ Vier Euro fünfzig.
  ● Gut, ich nehme das T-Shirt.
g ● Das kostet sechsundvierzig Euro?
    Nein, das ist zu teuer!
b € 67,50; *c* € 2,30; *e* € 40,00

5 *a* ● Ich möchte **drei Bananen**, **eine
      Ananas** und **ein halbes Kilo
      Tomaten.**
   ◆ **Sechs Euro fünfundsiebzig
      (€ 6,75)**, bitte.
b ● Ich möchte **eine Flasche
      Limonade, einen Karton Milch**
      und **ein Päckchen Kaffee.**
   ◆ **Elf Euro fünfzehn (€ 11,15)**,
      bitte.

6 *a* Gehen Sie hier rechts und nehmen
     Sie die dritte Straße links. Das ist
     dann links.
b Gehen Sie geradeaus. Nehmen
     Sie die zweite Straße links und dann
     die erste Straße links und dann ist
     es rechts.
c Gehen Sie geradeaus. Nehmen Sie
     die zweite Straße rechts und dann
     die erste Straße links. Das ist dann
     rechts.
*a shopping centre; b tourist office;
c cathedral*

7 *a* 1st; *b* 2nd; *c* 3rd; *d* ground floor;
   e basement

8 *a* der Sportabteilung; *b* dem
   Restaurant; *c* sind neben

9 *c* False: she has an office on the
   2nd floor.
   d False: he has an hour.
   f False: it's not far.

Unit 8

Page 72 Checking in at reception

2 ● Guten Tag. Ich heiße Friedmann,
   Martin Friedmann.
 ◆ Guten Tag, Herr Friedmann.
   Ein **Einzelzimmer** mit **Bad**,
   nicht wahr? Zimmer Nummer

siebenunddreißig (**37**). Hier ist der
Schlüssel.
● Guten Abend. Ich habe
   eine Reservierung für ein
   Doppelzimmer. Mein Name ist
   Doris Wolf.
◆ Ein **Doppelzimmer** mit
   Dusche, Frau Wolf, ja? … Hier
   ist der Schlüssel, Nummer
   hundertzwanzig (**120**).
● Guten Abend. Wie heißen Sie, bitte?
◆ Lange, Michael Lange. Ich
   habe eine Reservierung für ein
   Einzelzimmer.
● Oh ja, ein **Einzelzimmer** mit **Bad**.
   Zimmer Nummer vierundsechzig
   (**64**).

3 *a* ● Guten Tag. Ich heiße Anna
      Dürnbeck.
   ◆ Ach ja, ein **Einzelzimmer**,
      nicht wahr? Nummer fünfzig
      im **zweiten** Stock. Hier ist der
      Schlüssel.
b ● Guten Abend. Mein Name
      ist Fritz Auerbach. Ich habe
      eine Reservierung für ein
      Doppelzimmer im **Erdgeschoss**.
   ◆ Oh ja, Herr Auerbach, ein
      Doppelzimmer mit Bad.
c ● Guten Abend. Ich habe
      eine Reservierung für **ein
      Einzelzimmer mit Dusche.**
   ◆ Wie heißen Sie, bitte?
   ● Meyer, Heinrich.
   ◆ Ja, Zimmer hundertvierzehn im
      ersten Stock.
Heinrich Meyer (c) was asked his name.

Page 73 Asking for a hotel room

2 *a* ● Guten Tag. Haben Sie ein
      Zimmer frei?
   ◆ Möchten Sie ein Einzelzimmer
      oder ein Doppelzimmer?
   ● Ein Einzelzimmer mit Dusche **für
      zwei Nächte,** bitte.
b ● Guten Abend. Haben Sie ein
      Doppelzimmer frei?
   ◆ Für wie lange?
   ● **Für drei Nächte.**

c ● Guten Abend. Haben Sie ein
    Zimmer frei?
  ◆ Für heute oder …?
  ● Ja, **für heute.** Ein Einzelzimmer,
    bitte.
  a 2 nights; b 3 nights; c tonight

3 A, B, C, D, E, F, G, H, I, J, K, L, M, N,
  O, P, Q, R, S, T, U, V, W, X, Y, Z
  Ä, Ö, Ü
  KURT STOCKER
  Familienname: Stocker

4 a ● Wie heißen Sie, bitte?
    ◆ Henkel, Martha.
    ● Henkel, wie schreibt man das?
    ◆ **HENKEL.**
    ● Und Martha?
    ◆ **MARTHA.**
  b ● Guten Tag, ich habe eine
      Reservierung.
    ◆ Wie heißen Sie, bitte?
    ● Anja Weidmann.
    ◆ Wie schreibt man das?
    ● **WEIDMANN.**
    ◆ Und Anja?
    ● **ANJA.**
    ◆ Danke. Hier ist der Schlüssel.
  c ● Wie heißen Sie?
    ◆ Mein Familienname ist Schmid.
    ● **SCHMID.**
    ◆ Und der Vorname?
    ● Oskar.
    ◆ **OSKAR.**
    ● Ist gut, Herr Schmid. Danke.

5 Haben Sie ein Zimmer frei für heute?;
  Ein Einzelzimmer für vier Nächte,
  bitte; Haben Sie ein Doppelzimmer
  (frei) für drei Nächte?

Page 74 Booking ahead

2 a ● Hotel Sonne, guten Abend.
    ◆ Guten Abend. Ich möchte ein
      Doppelzimmer reservieren.
    ● Für wann?
    ◆ **Vom neunundzwanzigsten Juni
      bis zum zwölften Juli.**
    ● Ja, mit Bad oder mit Dusche?

b ● Guten Tag. Hotel Sonne.
  ◆ Guten Tag. Ich möchte ein
    Einzelzimmer **vom fünften bis
    zum achten März** reservieren.
  ● Es tut mir leid, das Hotel ist voll
    besetzt.
c ● Guten Tag. Hotel Sonne.
  ◆ Guten Tag. Haben Sie ein
    Doppelzimmer mit Dusche frei?
  ● Für wann?
  ◆ **Vom zweiten April bis zum
    vierten Mai.**
  ● Ja, wie heißen Sie, bitte?
  *a 29/6–12/7; b 5–8/3; c 2/4–4/5;
  customer b will be disappointed*

Page 75 Enquiring about facilities

2
a ● Wann ist Frühstück, bitte?
  ◆ Von sieben bis neun.
b ● Bis wann ist die Bar geöffnet?
  ◆ Die Bar? Bis elf Uhr.
c ● Gibt es ein Schwimmbad hier im
    Hotel?
  ◆ Nein, es tut mir leid. Es gibt ein
    Schwimmbad in der Nähe, neben
    dem Rathaus.
d ● Gibt es einen Parkplatz?
  ◆ Ja, es gibt einen Parkplatz hinter
    dem Hotel.
  *a When is breakfast?; b Until when is
  the bar open?; c Is there a swimming
  pool in the hotel?; d Is there a car park?*

3 *a From 7 till 9; b Until 11; c No, but
  there's one nearby, next to the town
  hall; e Yes, behind the hotel*

4 ● Hier ist das Hotel Sonne. Wir
    haben Zimmer **für drei Nächte.**
  ◆ Wann ist Frühstück?
  ● Frühstück ist **von sechs bis zehn**
    und das Restaurant ist abends **von
    sieben bis elf** geöffnet. Es gibt
    eine Bar **neben dem Restaurant
    im Erdgeschoss.**
  ◆ Bis wann ist die Bar geöffnet?
  ● Die Bar ist auch bis elf Uhr abends

geöffnet.

◆ Gibt es ein Schwimmbad?
● Ja, es gibt ein Schwimmbad **im Untergeschoss.**

a from 6 to 10 o'clock; b from 7 to 11p.m.; c ground floor, next to restaurant; d basement; They will be staying for 3 nights.

Page 76 Put it all together

1 Familienname: Kraus
   Vorname: Hans
   Beruf: Architekt
   Nationalität: Holländer
   Zimmernummer: 76 vom 11/9 bis zum 18/9

2 *a* ein Einzelzimmer mit Dusche;
   b einen Parkplatz; *c* Frühstück;
   d ersten bis zum vierten März

3 *a* When for?; *b* Have you a room?;
   c The hotel's full; *d* nearby; *e* behind the hotel; *f* For how long?

Page 77 Now you're talking!

1 ● Guten Tag. Kann ich Ihnen helfen?
   ◆ **Guten Tag. Haben Sie ein Zimmer frei?**
   ● Ein Einzelzimmer oder ein Doppelzimmer?
   ◆ **Ein Einzelzimmer mit Bad.**
   ● Für wie lange?
   ◆ **Für drei Nächte.**
   ● Gut. Also Zimmer dreiundneunzig im zweiten Stock.

2 ● **Guten Tag. Ich habe eine Reservierung.**
   ◆ Wie heißen Sie?
   ● **Ich heiße James Wilson.**
   ◆ Ein Doppelzimmer mit Dusche, nicht wahr?
   ● **Ja, vom neunzehnten bis zum sechsundzwanzigsten Juni.**
   ◆ Gut. Hier ist der Schlüssel, Herr Wilson.
   ● **Gibt es einen Parkplatz in der Nähe?**

◆ Ja, hinter dem Hotel.

3 ● Guten Morgen. Eurotel Dresden.
   ◆ **Guten Morgen. Ich möchte ein Zimmer reservieren.**
   ● Für wann?
   ◆ **Für heute.**
   ● Für wie lange?
   ◆ **Bis zum zwölften.**
   ● Ja, wie heißen Sie, bitte?
   ◆ **Ich heiße (your name).**
   ● Wie schreibt man das?
   ◆ **Spell your name.**

Page 78 Quiz

1 März; *2* 3rd to 9th May; *3* What time is breakfast?; *4* Gibt es ein Schwimmbad in der Nähe?;
5 Familienname; *6* five nights; *7* spell out what you just said; *8* regret

Unit 9

Pages 80 & 81 Asking about public transport and arrival and departure times

2 ● Welche Linie fährt zum Rathaus?
   ◆ Die Linie fünf.
   ● Welche Linie fährt zur Stadtmitte?
   ◆ Die Linie siebenundzwanzig.
   ● Welche Linie fährt nach Schwabing?
   ◆ Die Linie vierzehn.
   ● Welche Linie fährt zum Bahnhof?
   ◆ Die Linie zweiunddreißig oder die Linie acht.

   a 5, *town hall*; *b* 27, *town centre*;
   c 14, *Schwabing*; *d* 32 or 8, *station*

3 ● Fährt diese **Straßenbahn** zum Rathaus, bitte?
   ◆ Nein, **nach** Schwabing. Der Bus **fährt** zum Rathaus. Dort drüben ist die **Bushaltestelle.**
   ● Welche **Linie** fährt **zum** Rathaus?
   ◆ Die **Linie** fünf.

5 ● Der Zug nach Zürich fährt um siebzehn Uhr zwanzig ab.

- ◆ Der Intercity nach Leipzig fährt in zehn Minuten um acht Uhr zehn ab.
- ● Der Zug nach Wien kommt **um dreiundzwanzig Uhr vierzehn** in Linz an.
- ◆ Der Zug nach Siegen kommt um **fünfzehn Uhr dreißig** an.

Siegen: Ankunft 15:30
Linz: Ankunft 23:14
Zürich: Abfahrt 17:20
Leipzig: Abfahrt 8:10

6 ● Wann kommt der nächste Zug in Garmisch an?
- ◆ Um dreizehn Uhr dreißig.
- ● Wann kommt der Bus in Schwabing an?
- ◆ Um siebzehn Uhr fünfzehn.
- ● Wann fährt der Bus zum Stadion?
- ◆ Um neun Uhr zwanzig.
- ● Wann fährt die Straßenbahn Linie sechs zur Stadtmitte?
- ◆ Um zwanzig Uhr.
  Garmisch: 13:30; train
  Schwabing: 17:15; bus
  stadium: 9:20; bus
  town centre: 20.00; tram

Pages 82 & 83 Buying tickets and checking travel details

2 ● Einmal zweiter Klasse hin und zurück nach Innsbruck, bitte.
- ◆ Dreimal erster Klasse einfach nach Potsdam, bitte.
- ● Zweimal zweiter Klasse einfach nach Augsburg.
- ◆ Einmal zweiter Klasse hin und zurück nach Vaduz.
- ● Viermal zweiter Klasse einfach nach Basel, bitte.

Innsbruck: 1; 2nd; return
Potsdam: 3; 1st; single
Augsburg: 2; 2nd; single
Vaduz: 1; 2nd; return
Basel: 4; 2nd; single

3 *a* Zweimal erster Klasse einfach nach München, bitte.
b Einmal zweiter Klasse hin und zurück nach Innsbruck, bitte.
c Viermal zweiter Klasse einfach nach Mainz, bitte.
d Dreimal zweiter Klasse hin und

zurück nach Mannheim, bitte.

5 *a* ● Ich möchte nach Augsburg. Muss ich umsteigen?
- ◆ Ja, in München.
b ● Einmal einfach nach Hamburg, bitte. Kann ich einen Platz reservieren?
- ◆ Ja, sicher.
c ● Von welchem Gleis fährt der Zug nach Basel?
- ◆ Von Gleis 5B.
d ● Ich möchte nach Potsdam. Wo muss ich aussteigen?
- ◆ In Berlin.
a Augsburg; Do I have to change?
b Hamburg; Can I reserve a seat?
c Basel; What platform does the train go from?
e Potsdam; Where must I get off?

6 *a* Ja, in Köln; *b* Ja, sicher; *c* Von Gleis 7; *d* In Berlin.

7 ● Muss ich umsteigen?
- ● Von welchem Gleis fährt der Zug?
- ● Wo muss ich aussteigen?

Page 84 Put it all together

1 *A1* Einmal nach Bonn, bitte.
A2 Nach Bonn? Ja, einfach oder hin und zurück?
A3 Einfach, bitte.
A4 € 28,40 einmal einfach nach Bonn.
B1 Wann fährt der Bus zur Stadtmitte, bitte?
B2 Die Linie 7 zur Stadtmitte? Um 17:00.
B3 Und wo ist die Bushaltestelle für die Linie 7?
B4 Da drüben, gegenüber dem Rathaus.

2 *a* vierzehn Uhr vierzig; *b* sechzehn Uhr dreißig; *c* zwölf Uhr fünf; *d* sieben Uhr fünfzehn

3 *a* welchem; *b* Wann; *c* Wo; *d* Welche; *e* Wo

4 *a* nach; *b* zur; *c* zum; nach

Page 85 Now you're talking!

1 ● Der nächste Zug nach Bad Tölz fährt in zwanzig Minuten von Gleis

vier ab.

- ◆ **Wann fährt der nächste Zug nach Bad Tölz?**
- ● In zwanzig Minuten, um dreizehn Uhr fünfundzwanzig.
- ◆ **Von welchem Gleis fährt der Zug?**
- ● Von Gleis vier.
- ◆ **Einmal zweiter Klasse hin und zurück nach Bad Tölz, bitte.**

2 ● **Einmal zweiter Klasse einfach nach Hamburg, bitte.**
- ◆ Nach Hamburg?
- ● **Ja, was kostet es?**
- ◆ Es kostet neunzig Euro.
- ● **Kann ich einen Platz reservieren?**
- ◆ Ja, sicher.

3 ● **Wo ist die Bushaltestelle?**
- ◆ Gegenüber dem Rathaus.
- ● **Einmal hin und zurück, bitte. Was kostet es?**
- ◆ Das kostet zwölf Euro.
- ● **Wann fährt der nächste Bus?**
- ◆ Um zehn Uhr dreißig.
- ● **Wann kommt der Bus in Oberammergau an?**
- ◆ Er kommt um elf Uhr fünfzig an.
- ● **Wo muss ich aussteigen?**
- ◆ Am Marktplatz.
- ● **Ist es weit zum Stadttheater?**
- ◆ Nein, zehn Minuten zu Fuß.
- ● **Wann fährt der Bus nach München?**
- ◆ Der Bus fährt um … siebzehn Uhr fünfzehn.

Page 86 Quiz

1 change in Koblenz; *2* at the station; *3* Linie; *4* zum Bahnhof; *5* it's going to Bonn; *6* Ankunft; *7* mit der Straßenbahn; *8* einen Platz

Unit 10

Page 88 Reading the menu

2 ● Die Speisekarte, bitte.
- ◆ Bitte schön.
- ● Sauerbraten … Was für Fleisch ist das? Ist das Rindfleisch?
- ◆ Ja, das ist Rindfleisch.
- ● Und was ist Weißwurst?

- ◆ Weißwurst ist Kalbfleisch.
- ● Ist Jägerschnitzel Schweinefleisch oder Kalbfleisch?
- ◆ Jägerschnitzel ist Schweinefleisch.
Sauerbraten = beef; Weißwurst = veal; Jägerschnitzel = pork

3 *a* seafood; *b* seafood; *c* pork; *d* beef; *e* veal; *f* pork; *g* beef; *h* seafood

Page 89 Ordering a meal

2 ● Bitte schön?
- ◆ Was **empfehlen** Sie?
- ● Der Sauerbraten und das Hähnchen mit Salat sind **gut**.
- ◆ Ich nehme das Hähnchen.
- ● Und was ist die **Tagessuppe**?
- ◆ Tomatensuppe.
- ● Also eine Tomatensuppe und zwei Hähnchen.
'Salat' is salad.

3 ● Und zum Trinken?
- ◆ Ein Viertelliterglas Weißwein, bitte.
- ● Für mich eine Flasche Mineralwasser.
Helga: quarter litre glass of white wine; Kurt: bottle of mineral water

4 *a* ● Bitte schön?
    - ◆ Ich möchte Melone mit Schinken, bitte.
    - ● Und dann?
    - ◆ Schweinekotelett mit Salat.
  b ● Was empfehlen Sie?
    - ◆ Die Tagessuppe ist Tomatensuppe. Der Fisch und das Rumpsteak sind gut.
    - ● Gut. Ich nehme Fisch mit Pommes frites.
    - ◆ Und die Suppe?
    - ● Nein, danke.
  c ● Die Speisekarte, bitte.
    - ◆ Bitte schön.
    - ● Ich möchte Heringssalat und dann Hähnchen.
    - ◆ Mit Reis oder Pommes frites?
    - ● Mit Reis, bitte.
    - ◆ … Guten Appetit!
b; two; salad; c; rice

Page 90 Choosing cakes and desserts

2 ● Möchten Sie eine Nachspeise?
◆ Was für Nachspeisen gibt es?
● Na, es gibt gemischtes Eis, Schokoladentorte, Nusstorte, Käsekuchen, oder wir haben auch frisches Obst.
◆ Für mich **Käsekuchen**, bitte.
● Als Nachspeise nehme ich frisches Obst … nein, nein, **gemischtes Eis**.
◆ **Mit Sahne?**
● Ja, bitte.

3 ● Was möchten Sie, Claudia?
◆ Ich möchte ein Stück **Nusstorte mit Sahne**.
● Und Sie, Manfred?
◆ Für mich **Schokoladentorte**, aber keine Sahne.
● Und ich nehme ein Stück **Obsttorte** ohne Sahne.
◆ So, **ein Stück Nusstorte mit Sahne, einmal Schokotorte und einmal Obsttorte**. Und zum Trinken?
● Drei Tassen Kaffee, bitte.
Order c

Page 91 Finishing the meal

2 ● Die Rechnung, bitte.
◆ Ja, gut. Hat's geschmeckt?
● Ja, es hat gut geschmeckt.
◆ So, eine Tomatensuppe, zwei Hähnchen, Schokoladentorte, Käsekuchen, Weißwein und Mineralwasser – das macht siebenundzwanzig Euro dreißig. Zahlen Sie bitte an der Kasse.
● Das ist für Sie.
◆ Danke schön. Auf Wiedersehen.
a Schokoladentorte, Käsekuchen; b at the cash desk; c yes; d € 27,30

3 ● Die **Rechnung**, bitte.
◆ Ja, gut. Hat's **geschmeckt?**
● Ja, es hat **gut geschmeckt**. Was macht das?
◆ Das **macht** sechsunddreißig Euro.
● Danke. Das ist **für Sie**.
Was macht das? = What does it come to?

4 Die Rechnung, bitte; Das ist für Sie; Es hat gut geschmeckt.

Page 92 Put it all together

1 Vorspeisen: Heringssalat, Tomatensuppe, Tunfischsalat; Hauptgerichte: Schweinekotelett, Hähnchen, Rinderbraten, Kalbsleber; Nachspeisen: Käsekuchen, gemischtes Eis, Apfelkuchen, frisches Obst

2 1 e; 2 c; 3 g; 4 a; 5 d; 6 f; 7 b

3 *a* Einen Viertelliter Weißwein, bitte; *b* Ich nehme gemischtes Eis; *c* Es hat gut geschmeckt; *d* € 45,20; *e* Der Fisch ist gut; *f* Das ist Kalbfleisch.

Page 93 Now you're talking!

1 ● **Die Speisekarte, bitte.**
◆ Bitte schön.
● **Was für Fleisch ist das?**
◆ Eisbein – das ist Schweinefleisch.
● **Ich nehme Hähnchen mit Reis.**
◆ Und zum Trinken?
● **Ein Glas Mineralwasser, bitte.**

2 ● **Was empfehlen Sie?**
◆ Der Fisch ist heute sehr frisch.
● **Gut. Also der Fisch, bitte.**
◆ Mit Salat oder Pommes frites?
● **Ich möchte Salat.**

3 ● Guten Appetit! … Hat's geschmeckt?
◆ **Ja, es hat gut geschmeckt. Als Nachspeise nehme ich frisches Obst.**
● Und sonst noch etwas?
◆ **Ich möchte ein Kännchen Kaffee mit Sahne.**

4 ● Die Rechnung, bitte.
◆ Also … Fisch mit Salat, frisches Obst und ein Kännchen Kaffee … das macht dreizehn Euro sechzig. Zahlen Sie bitte an der Kasse.
● **Das ist für Sie.**
◆ Danke schön. Auf Wiedersehen.

Page 94 Quiz

1 Schweinekotelett; *2* Guten Appetit!; *3* Vorspeisen, Hauptgerichte, Nachspeisen; *4* Wiener Schnitzel; *5* Es hat gut geschmeckt; *6* Tomatensuppe; *7* pay; *8* when giving a tip

Kontrollpunkt 3

Pages 95–99

1 ● Guten Abend. Ich habe eine **Reservierung**.
 ◆ Wie **heißen Sie**, bitte?
 ● Mein **Name** ist (your name).
 ◆ Ach ja, ein Einzelzimmer mit Bad, nicht wahr?
 ● Nein, nein, ein Einzelzimmer **mit Dusche**.
 ◆ Oh, entschuldigen Sie, und bis wann?
 ● Bis **zum neunten**.

2 ◆ Kann ich Ihnen helfen?
 ◆ **Wann ist Frühstück, bitte?**
 ● Von sieben bis zehn.
 ◆ Und **wo ist die Bar?**
 ● Im Erdgeschoss neben dem Restaurant.
 ◆ Danke. Und **wann ist die Bar geöffnet?**
 ● Von drei Uhr nachmittags bis elf Uhr abends.
 ◆ **Gibt es ein Schwimmbad im Hotel?**
 ● Nein, es tut mir leid, aber es gibt ein Schwimmbad in der Nähe neben dem Museum.
 a from 7 until 10; b on the ground floor next to the restaurant; c from 3 p.m. until 11 p.m.; d no, but there is one nearby, next to the museum

3 *a* die Fähre; *b* kommt; *c* hin und zurück

4 Ich möchte Heringssalat; Hähnchen mit Reis, bitte; Ja, als Nachspeise nehme ich frisches Obst; *c* Guten Appetit!

5 Gehen Sie hier geradeaus, nehmen Sie die erste Straße links und dann die zweite Straße rechts.

6 ● Bitte schön?
 ◆ **Ich möchte eine Tasche. Was kosten sie?**
 ● Fünfundvierzig Euro (**€ 45**).
 ◆ **Die sind zu teuer.**
 ● Die Tasche hier ist schön und kostet siebenundzwanzig Euro fünfzig (**€ 27,50**).
 ◆ **Das ist schön. Ich nehme die Tasche.**
 ● Danke. Zahlen Sie bitte an der Kasse.
 ◆ **Kann ich mit Kreditkarte bezahlen?**
 ● Ja, sicher.

7 *a* ● **Wo wohnen Sie?**
 ◆ Ich wohne in Potsdam.
 b ● **Sind Sie verheiratet?**
 ◆ Ja, mein Mann heißt Martin.
 c ● **Haben Sie Kinder?**
 ◆ Ja, einen Sohn, Dieter, und eine Tochter, Undine.
 d ● **Wie alt ist Undine?**
 ◆ Sie ist fünfzehn.
 e ● **Wie alt ist Dieter?**
 ◆ Er ist achtzehn.
 f ● **Was sind Sie?**
 ◆ Ich bin Programmiererin und mein Mann ist Lehrer.
 g ● **Was möchten Sie?**
 ◆ Ein Glas Weißwein, bitte.
 h ● **Also ein Glas Weißwein und ein Glas Rotwein, bitte.**

8 *a* Haus Vogtland (Tuesday) and Rathauskeller (Monday); *b* in the market square; *c* in the old town, opposite the cathedral; *d* Rathauskeller; *e* Rathauskeller (Saturday and Sunday); *f* Haus Vogtland and Zum goldenen Löwen; *g* gloves: Lederwaren, 2nd; sausage: Lebensmittel, basement; notepaper: Schreibwaren, ground; chocolates: Süßwaren, ground; perfume: Parfum, 1st; *h* wine; *i* behind the town hall; *j* arrival at Neuschwanstein; *k* half an hour; *l* next to the post office

grammar

Grammar explains how a language works. When you're learning a new language it really helps to learn some basic rules, which are easier to follow if you understand these essential grammatical terms.

Nouns are the words for living beings, things, places and abstract concepts: *daughter, designer, Rachel, shark, hat, village, Berlin, measles, freedom.*

Articles are definite: <u>*the*</u> house, <u>*the*</u> houses, or indefinite: <u>*a*</u> house, <u>*an*</u> area.

Gender: in German every noun is masculine (m), feminine (f) or neuter (nt). This is its gender, and you need to know a noun's gender because words used with it, such as articles and adjectives, have corresponding masculine, feminine and neuter forms.

Singular means one; **plural** means more than one.

Cases show the role that a word plays in the sentence. Case affects nouns, pronouns, articles and adjectives. Different grammatical cases (**nominative, accusative, dative**) are indicated by different endings.

Pronouns are words that can replace nouns. The most commonly used pronouns are **personal pronouns**, e.g. *you, she, him, we, it, they, them.*

Adjectives are words that describe nouns and pronouns: <u>*good*</u> idea; <u>*strong red*</u> wine; *she's* <u>*tall*</u>; *it was* <u>*weird*</u>. In German, unlike English, their endings often vary according to what they're describing.

Agreement: when a German article is used with a noun, it has to agree with, i.e. match, that noun in terms of gender (m, f or nt), number (singular or plural) and case.

The **endings** of words are the final letter(s). In English, a verb ending in -*ed* tells you it happened in the past, and a noun with an added -*s* indicates a plural. Endings are much more widespread in German: many words, including adjectives and verbs, rely on endings to convey essential information.

Prepositions are words like *at, by, for, until* or *with* which introduce information regarding time, place, manner, purpose etc.

Verbs relate to doing and being, and are easy to recognise in English because you can put *to* in front of them: *to live, to be, to speak, to explore, to think, to have, to need.* This is the **infinitive** of the verb, the form you find in the dictionary. German infinitives usually end in **-en**.

Regular verbs follow a predictable pattern, e.g. *I work, I worked, I have worked*; whereas irregular verbs are not predictable, e.g. *I eat, I ate, I have eaten*, and so have to be learnt separately.

The subject of a sentence is whoever or whatever is carrying out the action of the verb: ***They** have two children, **Maria** is going to Berlin, **Apples** cost €3*.

The object of a sentence is at the receiving end of the verb. It can be direct: *They have **two children**,* or indirect: *I said 'hello' **to the children***.

G1 nouns

All German nouns, not just proper nouns (names of people and places), begin with a capital letter:

der Bus *the bus*; **die Frau** *the woman*; **das Haus** *the house*

Every German noun is one of three genders: masculine (m), feminine (f), or neuter (nt). The nouns for male and female people are usually masculine and feminine: **der Mann** *man,* **die Mutter** *mother,* **der Kollege** *male colleague,* **die Kollegin** *female colleague*. This is not always the case, however: **die Person** (f) *person,* **das Mädchen** (nt) *girl,* **das Kind** (nt) *child*.

There's no means of telling the gender of most nouns from their meaning, and there often seems no logic to it: *knife* is neuter (**das Messer**), *fork* is feminine (**die Gabel**), and *spoon* is masculine (**der Löffel**). The best thing to do is to learn the gender of new words as you meet them by learning the noun together with **der** (m), **die** (f) or **das** (nt). Don't learn vocabulary by saying *station* – **Bahnhof**, *cup* – **Tasse**, *child* – **Kind**, say *station* – **der Bahnhof**, *cup* – **die Tasse**, *child* – **das Kind**. Most of the time you'll be understood if you use a wrong gender, but a few nouns have different meanings depending on gender: **der See** *lake,* **die See** *sea*.

G2 grammatical case

Words have different endings in a German sentence according to whether they're the subject or the object of the verb, or whether they follow a particular preposition. These are known as ***case endings*** and they affect articles, adjectives, pronouns and sometimes nouns. There are four grammatical cases in German, three of which feature in this book. These are:
nominative, the form found in a dictionary: used for the subject of a sentence and after the verb *to be*.

Das Haus ist groß. *The house is big.*
Das ist mein Freund. *That is my friend.*

accusative: used for the direct object of a sentence.
Ich habe ein großes Haus. *I have a big house.*
Kennen Sie meinen Freund? *Do you know my friend?*

dative: used for the indirect object of the sentence.
Geben Sie es meinem Freund. *Give it to my friend.*
Wie geht es Ihnen? *How are you?* (lit. *How goes it to you?*)

G3 plural nouns

Making German nouns plural is not just a matter of adding **-s** as in English. German nouns add one of several different endings, and some nouns don't change at all.

Since the plural of German nouns is often unpredictable and unguessable, most dictionaries indicate the plural ending next to the singular, as does the glossary at the back of this book for plurals appearing in the units. You might see this in a dictionary: **die Frau (-en)**, **das Geschenk (-e)**. This means the plural of **Frau** is **Frauen** and the plural of **Geschenk** *present* is **Geschenke**.

masculine nouns
Most masculine nouns add an **-e**, or remain the same. The vowels **a**, **o**, or **u** might also add an umlaut. A few masculine nouns add **-n/-en** in the plural.

(ein) Tag (-e) *day*	→	**Tage** *days*
(ein) Apfel (-¨) *apple*	→	**Äpfel** *apples*
(ein) Sohn (-¨e) *son*	→	**Söhne** *sons*
(ein) Junge (-n) *boy*	→	**Jungen** *boys*
(ein) Tourist (-en)	→	**Touristen** *tourists*

feminine nouns
Most feminine nouns add **-n**, **-en**, or **-e** plus an umlaut. Feminine nouns ending **-in** add **-nen**.

(eine) Tomate (-n)	→	**Tomaten** *tomatoes*
(eine) Stadt (-¨e)	→	**Städte** *towns*
(eine) Zeitung (-en)	→	**Zeitungen** *newspapers*
(eine) Studentin (-nen)	→	**Studentinnen** *female students*

neuter nouns

Most neuter nouns add **-e** (but no umlaut), **-er** plus an umlaut, or they stay the same.

(ein) Jahr (-e)	→	**Jahre** *years*
(ein) Kind (-er)	→	**Kinder** *children*
(ein) Haus (-¨er)	→	**Häuser** *houses*
(ein) Buch (-¨er)	→	**Bücher** *books*
(ein) Brötchen (-)	→	**Brötchen** *rolls*
(ein) Zimmer (-)	→	**Zimmer** *rooms*

Words which have been adopted from English or French add an **-s**.

(ein) Hobby (-s)	→	**Hobbys**
(eine) Party (-s)	→	**Partys**
(ein) Club (-s)	→	**Clubs**
(ein) Taxi (-s)	→	**Taxis**

An exception is **(ein) Computer (-)** → **Computer** *computers*

G4 articles

In German, the words for *the* (definite article), and *a* (indefinite article) depend on whether the noun they are accompanying is masculine, feminine or neuter, singular or plural, and also whether it is nominative, accusative or dative.

definite article

	masculine singular	feminine singular	neuter singular	plural
nominative	**der**	**die**	**das**	**die**
accusative	**den**	**die**	**das**	**die**
dative	**dem**	**der**	**dem**	**den**

Ich nehme den Salat/die Kirschen. *I'll have the salad/the cherries.*
Möchten Sie Eis mit den Kirschen? *Would you like ice cream with the cherries?*

Unlike English, German uses the definite article with means of transport: **mit dem Bus** *by bus*; **mit der Straßenbahn** *by tram*.

Test your knowledge with our online quiz at
www.bbcactivelanguages.com/GermanGrammarQuiz

indefinite article

	masculine singular	feminine singular	neuter singular
nominative	ein	eine	ein
accusative	einen	eine	ein
dative	einem	einer	einem

Ich möchte einen Kaffee und ein Stück Torte. *I'd like a coffee and a piece of cake.*

Sie arbeitet in einer Bank. *She works in a bank.*

Ein(e) has no plural: **Ich möchte Äpfel** *I'd like (some) apples.*

Unlike English, German doesn't use the article with occupations.

Er ist Lehrer. *He is a teacher.*   **Sie ist Journalistin.** *She is a journalist.*

Mein *my*, **dein** *your* (familiar, singular), **sein** *his/its* work in exactly the same way as **ein**, as does **kein** *no, not a, not any*. These words, unlike **ein**, have a plural form:

nominative plural	accusative plural	dative plural
meine, keine etc	**meine, keine** etc	**meinen, keinen** etc

Ich habe kein Auto. *I haven't got a car.*
Es gibt keine Orangen. *There are no oranges.*
Ich besuche meinen Sohn. *I'm visiting my son.*
Hans arbeitet mit seinen Eltern. *Hans works with his parents.*

Ihr *her*, **unser** *our*, **euer** *your* (familiar, plural), **ihr** *their* and **Ihr** *your* (polite, singular and plural) also use the same endings:

Sie wohnt mit ihrer Schwester. *She lives with her sister.*

G5 adjectives

In German, if an adjective follows the verb *to be*, it is always in its dictionary form and never changes.

Unser Haus ist klein. *Our house is small.*
Meine Schuhe sind neu. *My shoes are new.*

If the adjective comes before the noun it describes, it must agree with that noun, which means that its ending will change depending on whether the noun is masculine, feminine or neuter, singular or plural, and also whether it is nominative, accusative or dative.

In addition, there are different sets of endings for adjectives that come after a definite article, an indefinite article, and for adjectives without an article.

adjective endings after the definite article

	masculine singular	feminine singular	neuter singular	plural
nominative	(der) -e	(die) -e	(das) -e	(die) -en
accusative	(den) -en	(die) -e	(das) -e	(die) -en
dative	(dem) -en	(der) -en	(dem) -en	(den) -en

adjective endings after the indefinite article, kein, and possessives

	masculine singular	feminine singular	neuter singular	plural
nom	(ein) -er	(eine) -e	(ein) -es	(keine) -en
acc	(einen) -en	(eine) -e	(ein) -es	(keine) -en
dat	(einem) -en	(einer) -en	(einem) -en	(keinen) -en

adjective endings for stand-alone adjectives without an article

	masculine singular	feminine singular	neuter singular	plural
nominative	-er	-e	-es	-e
accusative	-en	-e	-es	-e
dative	-em	-er	-em	-en

Das kleine weiße Haus. *The small white house.*
Ein kleines weißes Haus. *A small white house.*
Ich trinke deutsches Bier/deutschen Wein. *I drink German beer/wine.*
Mit meinem guten Freund. *With my good friend.*
Mit guten Freunden. *With good friends.*

It looks complicated, but there are patterns: the letter **r** is associated with masculine nominative and feminine dative singular, **s** is associated with neuter nominative and accusative, **m** with masculine and neuter dative. One of the words in the adjectival phrase will always include this key letter; if it isn't the article it will be the adjective: **der gute Wein**, **das gute Bier** (**r**, **s** on article); (**ein**) **guter Wein**, (**ein**) **gutes Bier** (**r**, **s** on adjective).

The basic form of the adjective is also the adverb. German adverbs don't add *-ly*, as in English: **gut** is *good* or *well*; **schnell** is *quick* or *quickly*.

G6 prepositions

Prepositions are words such as *in*, *from*, *to*, *of*, *without*. In German, prepositions are followed by specific cases.

prepositions followed by the accusative case:

bis *until*   **für** *for*   **ohne** *without*   **um** *at, round*

ein Geschenk für meinen Sohn *a present for my son*
bis nächste Woche *until next week*
rechts um die Ecke *round the corner on the right*

prepositions followed by the dative case:

aus *from*	**bei** *at, for* (working)
gegenüber *opposite*	**hinter** *behind*
mit *with, by* (transport)	**nach** *after, to* (towns, most countries)
neben *next to*	**von** *from*
zu *to*	

gegenüber der Post *opposite the post office*
mit dem Zug *by train*

Some prepositions relating to location can be followed by either the accusative case or the dative. Where there is no movement, the dative case is used; the accusative signifies movement.

an *at*   **auf** *on, onto*   **hinter** *behind*   **in** *in, into*

Ich wohne in der Stadt *I live in the town.*
Ich gehe in die Stadt *I'm going into town.*

Certain prepositions usually combine with the definite article:

an dem Montag	→	**am Montag** *on Monday*
in dem Hotel	→	**im Hotel** *in the hotel*
von dem dritten August	→	**vom dritten August** *from the third of August*
zu dem Bahnhof	→	**zum Bahnhof** *to the station*
zu der Stadtmitte	→	**zur Stadtmitte** *to the town centre*

Prepositions rarely correspond exactly between English and German, so it's best to learn set phrases as a whole:

zu Fuß *on foot*   **mit der Fähre** *by ferry*
im zweiten Stock *on the second floor*

G7 verbs

The infinitives of most German verbs end in **-en**. This is the form that you find in the dictionary, and is the equivalent of the English *to ...*: **wohnen** *to live*, **gehen** *to go*, **finden** *to find*. Removing the **-en** leaves you with the verb stem: **wohn**, **geh**, **find**. Other endings can then be added to the stem to agree with the subject, a noun or a personal pronoun, to convey specific information: **ich wohne** *I live*; **Maria geht** *Maria is going*; **sie finden** *they find*.

G8 regular verbs: present tense

This set of endings indicates that the verb is happening at the present time, conveying the English *I live*, *I'm living* and *I do live*.

		wohnen *to live*	**finden** *to find*
ich	*I*	wohn**e**	find**e**
du	*you*	wohn**st**	find**est**
er	*he, it (m)*	wohn**t**	find**et**
sie	*she, it (f)*		
es	*it*		
wir	*we*	wohn**en**	find**en**
ihr	*you*	wohn**t**	find**et**
sie	*they*	wohn**en**	find**en**
Sie	*you*	wohn**en**	find**en**

-e- is inserted for ease of pronunciation after stems ending in certain letters, such as **d** and **t** in the **du**, **er/sie/es** and **ihr** forms.

There are three words for *you*, and the verb has a different ending depending on which one you're using:

du *you*: someone you call by their first name
ihr *you*: two or more people you call by their first names
Sie *you*: the polite form, for one person or more than one, is used to address people you don't know well. **Sie** is always written with a capital **S**, to distinguish it from **sie** *they*.

Man means *one, you, we* or *they*, when no-one in particular is meant. It takes the same endings as **er, sie, es**:
Man findet leicht einen Parkplatz. *You'll easily find a car park./It's easy to find a car park.*

Other common verbs that are regular in the present tense include:

antworten *to answer*	**arbeiten** *to work*	**besuchen** *to visit*
fragen *to ask*	**heißen** *to be called*	**kaufen** *to buy*
kommen *to come*	**lernen** *to learn*	**machen** *to make, do*
regnen *to rain*	**reisen** *to travel*	**reservieren** *to reserve*
schließen *to close*	**schreiben** *to write*	**schwimmen** *to swim*
spielen *to play*	**stehen** *to stand*	**suchen** *to look for*
verstehen *to understand*	**warten** *to wait*	

ich frage *I ask*   **es regnet** *it's raining*
sie schreiben *they write*   **wir kommen** *we're coming*
Sie arbeiten *you work*   **sie antwortet** *she answers*
er versteht *he understands*

G9 verbs with a change of stem
Some **du** and **er/sie/es** verb forms undergo a change in the stem. The vowel either adds an umlaut or changes to a different vowel, and there may be other spelling changes.

	nehmen *to take*	**fahren** *to travel*	**geben** *to give*	**sprechen** *to speak*
ich	nehme	fahre	gebe	spreche
du	ni**mm**st	f**ä**hrst	gi**b**st	spri**ch**st
er, sie, es	ni**mm**t	f**ä**hrt	gibt	spricht
wir	nehmen	fahren	geben	sprechen
ihr	nehmt	fahrt	gebt	sprecht
sie Sie	nehmen nehmen	fahren fahren	geben geben	sprechen sprechen

Other common verbs with a change of stem in the **du** and **er/sie/es** forms include:

empfehlen *to recommend* **(empfiehlst, empfiehlt); essen** *to eat* **(isst, isst); fallen** *to fall* **(fällst, fällt); halten** *to hold, stop* **(hältst, hält); helfen** *to help* **(hilfst, hilft); laufen** *to run* **(läufst, läuft); lesen** *to read* **(liest, liest); schlafen** *to sleep* **(schläfst, schläft); sehen** *to see* **(siehst, sieht); versprechen** *to promise* **(versprichst, verspricht).**

Meine Tochter hilft. *My daughter helps.*
Er empfiehlt das Schnitzel. *He recommends the cutlet.*

G10 key irregular verbs
A few of the most commonly used verbs are irregular, i.e. they don't follow the regular patterns and have to be learnt separately.

	sein *to be*	**haben** *to have*
ich	**bin**	**habe**
du	**bist**	**hast**
er, sie, es	**ist**	**hat**
wir	**sind**	**haben**
ihr	**seid**	**habt**
sie Sie	**sind** **sind**	**haben** **haben**

	müssen *to have to, must*	**können** *to be able to, can*	**dürfen** *to be allowed*
ich	**muss**	**kann**	**darf**
du	**musst**	**kannst**	**darfst**
er, sie, es	**muss**	**kann**	**darf**
wir	**müssen**	**können**	**dürfen**
ihr	**müsst**	**könnt**	**dürft**
sie Sie	**müssen** **müssen**	**können** **können**	**dürfen** **dürfen**

Müssen, können and **dürfen** are known grammatically as modal verbs.
Ich möchte *I would like* is from the modal verb **mögen** *to like*, but not from the present tense:
Ich möchte ein Zimmer reservieren. *I'd like to book a room.*

G11 asking questions

German yes/no questions don't use extra words like *do* or *does*: you simply reverse the order of subject and verb.

Sie verstehen mich. *You understand me.*
Verstehen Sie mich? *Do you understand me?*
Herr und Frau Schmidt wohnen in Berlin. *Mr. and Mrs. Schmidt live in Berlin.*
Wohnen Herr und Frau Schmidt in Berlin? *Do Mr. and Mrs. Schmidt live in Berlin?*

G12 negatives

Do and *does* are not used in negatives either. To negate a verb, adverb or prepositional phrase, use **nicht**.

Ich verstehe Sie nicht. *I don't understand you.*
Er kommt morgen nicht. *He isn't coming tomorrow.*
Wir kommen nicht aus London. *We don't come from London.*
Die Bank ist nicht weit von der Post. *The bank is not far from the post office.*

To negate a noun and say *no/not any*, use **kein**. **Kein** takes the same endings as **ein**, but unlike **ein** has plural forms (see **articles**, page 121).

Ich habe keine Kinder. *I haven't any children./I have no children.*
Es gibt keinen Fisch. *There is no fish./There isn't any fish.*

G13 unique German features

Certain aspects of the German alphabet and language structure appear unfamiliar to English speakers. Some features unique to German are:

G14 umlauts

Three vowels can take an umlaut: **ä**, **ö** and **ü**. The umlaut changes the sound of the original vowel, because the tip of the tongue is further forward in the mouth when it is pronounced. The umlaut can change the meaning; in particular it often indicates the plural:

schon *already*; **schön** *beautiful*
Apfel *apple*; **Äpfel** *apples*
Mutter *mother*; **Mütter** *mothers*

When texting or emailing **ä**, **ö** and **ü** can be written **ae**, **oe** and **ue**. The URL for the newspaper **Süddeutsche Zeitung** is **sueddeutsche.de**.

G15 ß

The **ß** is pronounced *ss* and can only be written in the lower case. The German name for this letter is **eszett** or **scharfes s**. It is written after long vowels and diphthongs, whilst **ss** is written after short vowels:

Straße *street*   **Fuß** *foot*   **weiß** *white*   **Fluss** *river*   **dass** *that*

G16 word order

Except in yes/no questions, the verb is the second 'idea' in a sentence:

Meine Schwester | kommt | heute. *My sister is coming today.*
Heute | kommt | meine Schwester. *My sister is coming today.*
Welche Linie | fährt | zum Bahnhof? *Which number (bus, tram) goes to the station?*
Fährt | diese Straßenbahn | zum Bahnhof? *Does this tram go to the station?*

Modal verbs, e.g. **können** *can*, **müssen** *must*, and **dürfen** *to be allowed to*, send the verb they accompany, which is in the infinitive, to the end of the sentence.

Kann ich einen Platz reservieren? *Can I book a seat?*
Sie müssen in Köln umsteigen. *You must change (trains) in Cologne.*

G17 separable verbs

Some German verbs begin with a separable prefix (e.g. **ab-, an-, aus-, ein-, vor-**). In the present tense, this prefix usually separates from the main verb and moves to the end of the sentence:

Der Zug kommt um vier Uhr an. *The train arrives at four o'clock.*
Sie steigen am Marktplatz aus. *You get off at the market square.*

Common separable verbs are:

abfahren *to leave*	**ankommen** *to arrive*
anrufen *to telephone*	**aussteigen** *to get off*
einlösen *to cash*	**einsteigen** *to get on*
umsteigen *to change* (trains)	**vorstellen** *to introduce*

After modal verbs the prefix and main verb join up again at the end of the sentence:

Sie müssen am Marktplatz aussteigen. *You must get off at the market square.*

German is renowned for its long words. When it combines words, it usually doesn't hyphenate, it tags one directly on to another.

der Apfelsaft *apple juice* **Apfel** *apple* + **Saft** *juice*
die Kreditkarte *credit card* **Kredit** *credit* + **Karte** *card*
die Lederwarenabteilung *leather goods department*
Leder *leather* + **Waren** *goods* + **Abteilung** *department*

This can sometimes lead to three consecutive identical consonants:

die Schifffahrt *shipping* **Schiff** *ship* + **Fahrt** *journey*
der Balletttänzer *ballet dancer* **Ballett** *ballet* + **Tänzer** *dancer*

Sounds/letters are sometimes inserted:

das Schweinefleisch *pork* **Schwein** *pig* + **Fleisch** *meat*
das Einkaufszentrum *shopping centre* **Einkauf** *shopping* + **Zentrum** *centre*

The longest word in the German dictionary is:

Kraftfahrzeughaftpflichtversicherung, with 36 letters. It means *automobile liability insurance*, and is made up of **Kraftfahrzeug** *motor vehicle*, which itself is made up of **Kraft** *power* + **fahr** *travelling* + **Zeug** *equipment*, followed by **Haft**, a noun prefix + **Pflicht** *compulsory* + **Versicherung** *insurance*.

In German these long compound words are known as **Bandwurmwörter**, or *tapeworm words*.

The gender of compound nouns is determined by the final element:

die Bahn (f) *rail* so, **die Straßenbahn** (f) *tram*
but **der Bahnhof** (m) *station*, as the final element is **der Hof** (m), lit. *yard*
der Kaffee (m) + **die Pause** (f) → **die Kaffeepause** (f) *coffee break*
die Stadt (f) + **das Theater** (nt) → **das Stadttheater** (nt) *civic theatre*
Numbers combine to form compound words, too:
hundertsechsundvierzig Euro *146 euros*
zweihundertfünfzig Gramm *250 grams*

The increasing influence of English has meant that hyphens are now creeping into compound words, particularly where at least one of the elements is a word of foreign origin:

die Notebook-Tasche *case for a notebook computer*
Purists still insist that **Notebooktasche** is correct.

wordpower

Despite the uniqueness of some aspects of German, there are many similarities between English and German, since both belong to the same family of languages. The spelling of some words might not be identical but the meaning becomes clear when you say them:

Fisch	**Buch**	**Haus**
Bier	**Wein**	**Schuh**

If you take off the German verb ending **-(e)n**, the verb is often identical, or very similar, to the English:

beginnen	**finden**	**kosten**
lernen	**parken**	**singen**
sinken	**wandern**	**waschen**

In writing, the key to understanding many hundreds of German words lies in knowing how certain consonant sounds correspond between German and English:

b	→ *f, v*	**Silber, halb, sieben**
ch	→ *gh*	**Nacht, Licht, Tochter, lachen**
ch	→ *k*	**Milch, Buch, machen, brechen**
d	→ *th*	**danke, drei, Ding, Bad, Bruder, Leder**
f(f)	→ *p*	**helfen, Bischof, Schiff**
g	→ *y*	**Tag, Weg**
k	→ *c*	**Kino, Keller, kalt, Kaffee, Kreditkarte**
pf	→ *p(p)*	**Apfel, Pfanne**
sch	→ *s, sh*	**Fisch, schwimmen, falsch**
ss, ß	→ *t(t)*	**besser, Wasser, Fuß**
t	→ *d*	**hart, gut, Wort, Brot, Bett, Tochter**
v	→ *f*	**Vater, vier, voll, Volk**
z, tz	→ *t*	**Salz, Zunge, zehn, zu, Katze, sitzen**

Many English nouns and adjectives are used routinely in German, particularly relating to business e.g. **Marketing**, **Manager**, **Meeting**; and technology e.g. **Internet**, **Laptop**, **Tablet**, **Blog**, **Software**, **Website**, **Smartphone**, **online**. Verbs are given German endings: **downloaden**, **canceln**, **klicken**, **mailen**.

Not all such German nouns mean what they appear to mean: **ein Handy** is a mobile phone and **ein Dressman** is a male model.

top ten essentials

1 Describing and commenting:
   Das ist zu teuer! *It's too expensive!/That's too expensive!*
   Das ist nicht gut. *That isn't good.*

2 Talking about what's available:
   Es gibt warmes Wasser. *There's warm water.*
   Gibt es kein warmes Wasser? *Is there no warm water?*
   Es gibt deutsche Gerichte. *There are German dishes.*

3 Talking about having:
   Ich habe einen Sohn. *I have a son.*
   Haben Sie ein Zimmer? *Do you have a room?*
   Wir haben Ledertaschen. *We have some leather bags.*

4 Asking what things are:
   Was ist das? *What is that?*
   Was sind das? *What are they/those?*
   Wie schreibt man das? *How do you spell that?*

5 Asking where things are:
   Wo ist der Parkplatz? *Where is the car park?*
   Wo sind die Toiletten? *Where are the toilets?*

6 Saying you would like (to do) something:
   Ich möchte einen Kaffee. *I'd like a coffee.*
   Wir möchten Kaffee trinken. *We'd like to drink some coffee.*

7 Saying/asking if you can do something:
   Kann ich mit Kreditkarte bezahlen? *Can I pay with a credit card?*
   Wir können am Montag kommen. *We can come on Monday.*

8 Asking if you have to do something:
   Muss ich hier rechts gehen? *Do I have to turn right here?*
   Müssen wir umsteigen? *Do we have to change (trains)?*

9 Asking somebody to do something:
   Bitte wiederholen Sie! *Please could you say that again?*
   Sprechen Sie langsamer, bitte! *Could you speak more slowly, please?*
   ... ich verstehe nicht. *I don't understand.*

10 Imposing and apologising:
   Entschuldigen Sie bitte. *Excuse me please.*
   Es tut mir leid. *I'm sorry.*

German–English glossary

A

der Abend evening; guten
Abend good evening
aber but
abfahren to leave
die Abfahrt departure
die Abteilung department
acht eight
achtzehn eighteen
achtzig eighty
alles everything, all
alt old
die Altstadt old (part of)
town
der Amerikaner/die
Amerikanerin American
man/woman
an at
die Ananas pineapple
ankommen to arrive
die Ankunft arrival
anrufen to telephone
antworten to answer
der Apfel (pl Äpfel) apple
der Apfelkuchen apple
cake
der Apfelsaft apple juice
die Apotheke chemist's
der April April
arbeite (arbeiten) (I)
work (to work)
arbeitslos unemployed
der Architekt architect
auch also, too
auf Deutsch in German
auf Wiedersehen
goodbye
der Aufschnitt cold meats
der August August
aus from, out of
die Auskunft information
der Ausländer/die
Ausländerin foreigner
(m/f)

aussteigen to get off
(transport)
der Australier/die
Australierin Australian
man/woman
das Auto car

B

das Bad bath
der Bahnhof (railway)
station
die Banane (pl Bananen)
banana
die Bank bank
die Bar bar
Basel Basle
der Bayer Bavarian (man)
Bayerisch Bavarian
(dialect)
bei (working) for; at
der Beruf occupation
besetzt occupied; voll
besetzt fully booked
(hotel)
besuchen to visit
der Besucher visitor (m)
bezahlen to pay
das Bier beer
bin (sein) (I) am (to be)
bis until, to; bis zum until
the (date)
bitte please; don't
mention it
bitte schön here you are
bitte schön? can I help
you?
Bozen Bolzano
das Brötchen (pl
Brötchen) (bread) roll
der Brunnen fountain
das Buch (pl Bücher)
book
das Büro office
der Bus bus
die Bushaltestelle bus
stop

C

der Campingplatz
campsite
der Cent (pl Cent) cent
der Club (pl Clubs) club
die Cola coke (drink)
der Computer (pl
Computer) computer

D

da there
der Dampfer steamer
danke thanks, thank you
danke schön thank you
(very much)
dann then
darf (dürfen) (I) may (to
be allowed); darf ich …?
may I …?
das that, the (nt); das ist
that is; das macht … that
comes to …; das sind
these are
dass that (conjunction)
dein, deine your
der the (m)
deutsch German
der Deutsche/die
Deutsche German man/
woman
das Deutschland
Germany
der Dezember December
die the (f or pl); die sind
they/those are
der Dienstag Tuesday
dieser, diese, dieses this
der Dom cathedral
der Donnerstag Thursday
das Doppelzimmer
double room
dort there; dort drüben
over there
die Dose tin, can

drei three
dreimal three times
dreißig thirty
dreizehn thirteen
dritte third; im dritten Stock on the third floor
die Dusche shower
du you (informal singular)
dürfen to be allowed to

E

ebenfalls likewise
die Ecke corner
ein, eine a, an, one
einfach single (ticket)
das Einkaufszentrum shopping centre
einlösen to cash (a cheque)
einmal once
eins one
einsteigen to get on
das Einzelzimmer single room
das Eis ice cream
das Eisbein knuckle of pork
elf eleven
die Eltern (pl) parents
empfehlen to recommend
empfiehlt (he/she/it) recommends
England (nt) England
der Engländer/die Engländerin English man/ woman
entschuldigen Sie excuse me
er he
das Erdgeschoss ground floor
erste first; die erste Straße the first road/ street
erster Klasse first class (ticket)
im ersten Stock on the first floor

es it; es freut mich pleased to meet you
es gibt there is, there are
essen to eat
es tut mir leid I'm sorry
etwas something, anything
euer, eure your (pl)
der Euro (pl Euro) euro

F

die Fähre ferry
die Fahrkarte ticket
fahre (fahren) (I) travel (to travel)
fährt (he/she/it) travels
der Familienname surname
der Familienstand marital status
der Februar February
finde (finden) (I) find (to find)
der Fisch fish
die Flasche bottle
der Fluss river
fragen to ask
das Frankreich France
die Frau wife, woman, Mrs
die Frauenmode women's fashions
frei free, vacant
der Freitag Friday
fremd strange
der Freund (pl Freunde) friend
freut mich pleased to meet you
frisch fresh; frisches Obst fresh fruit
das Frühstück breakfast
fünf five
fünfzehn fifteen
fünfzig fifty
für for
der Fuß foot; zu Fuß on foot

G

die Gabel fork
das Gasthaus pub
geben to give
gegenüber opposite
gehen to go
das Geld money
gemischt mixed; gemischtes Eis mixed ice cream
geöffnet open
geradeaus straight on
das Gericht (pl Gerichte) dish
gern I'd love to, willingly
das Geschenk (pl Geschenke) present (gift)
geschlossen closed
gibt (geben) (he/she/it) gives (to give)
das Glas glass
das Gleis platform
das Gramm gram
groß big
Grüß Gott! Hello!
gut good, well; Gute Nacht! Goodnight!
Guten Abend! Good evening!
Guten Appetit! Enjoy your meal!
Guten Morgen! Good morning!
Guten Tag! Good day!, Good afternoon!

H

habe (haben) (I) have (to have)
das Hähnchen chicken
halb half; ein halbes Kilo half a kilo
hält (he/she/it) holds, stops
halten to hold, stop
hat (haben) (it) has (to have); es hat gut

geschmeckt it was good; hat's geschmeckt? did you enjoy your meal?

der Hauptbahnhof main station

das Hauptgericht (pl Hauptgerichte) main course

das Haus (pl Häuser) house

die Hausfrau housewife

die Haushaltswarenabteilung household goods department

heiße (heißen) (I) am called (to be called)

helfen to help

der Heringssalat herring salad

der Herr Mr

heute today

hier here

hilft (helfen) (he/she/it) helps (to help)

hin und zurück return (ticket)

hinter behind

das Hobby (pl Hobbys) hobby

der Holländer Dutchman

das Hotel hotel

hundert (a) hundred

I

ich I

Ihnen (to) you (formal singular and plural)

ihr you (informal plural)

Ihr, Ihre your (formal singular and plural)

ihr, ihre her, its, their

im in the (m/nt)

in in, into; in der Nähe nearby

internationale international

der Ire Irishman

die Irin Irishwoman

das Irland Ireland

isst (essen) (he/she/it) eats (to eat)

ist (sein) (he/she/it) is (to be)

der Italiener/die Italienerin Italian man/woman

J

ja yes

das Jägerschnitzel pork cutlet with peppers and mushrooms

das Jahr (pl Jahre) year; … Jahre alt … years old

der Januar January

die Journalistin journalist (f)

der Juli July

der Junge (pl Jungen) boy

der Juni June

K

der Kaffee coffee

das Kalbfleisch veal

die Kalbsleber calf's liver

der Kanadier/die Kanadierin Canadian man/woman

kann (können) (I) can (to be able to)

das Kännchen pot, jug

der Karton carton

der Käse cheese

der Käsekuchen cheesecake

die Kasse till, cash desk

kaufen to buy

das Kaufhaus department store

kein, keine not a, not any

die Kekse (pl) biscuits

die Kellnerin (f) waitress

kennen (kennen) (you) know (to know)

das Kilo kilo(gram)

das Kind (pl Kinder) child

der Kinderspielplatz children's playground

die Kirsche (pl Kirschen) cherry

das Kirschwasser cherry brandy

klein small

der Knoblauch garlic

der Kollege/die Kollegin colleague (m/f)

Köln Cologne

komme (kommen) (I) come (to come)

kommt … an (ankommen) (it) arrives (to arrive)

die Konditorei cake shop

können to be able to

der Kontrollpunkt checkpoint

kostet (kosten) (it) costs (to cost)

der Krabbencocktail prawn cocktail

die Kreditkarte credit card

der Kunde customer (m)

die Kundin customer (f)

L

das Land country, German state

langer Samstag 'long Saturday'

langsam slow(ly)

laufen to run

läuft (he/she/it) runs

die Lebensmittelabteilung food hall

die Leber liver

die Ledertasche (pl Ledertaschen) leather bag

die Lederwarenabteilung leather goods department

der Lehrer teacher (m)

die Lehrerin teacher (f)

leicht easily

lernen to learn
lesen to read
liest (he/she/it) reads
die Limonade lemonade
die Linie line
links left, to the left
der Liter litre
der Löffel spoon
lokale local
das Lotto bingo

M

machen to make, to do
das Mädchen girl
der Mai May
man you, one; man schreibt you write/spell
der Mann man; husband
die Männermode men's fashions
der Marktplatz market square
der März March
der Mechaniker (m) mechanic
die Mechanikerin (f) mechanic
mein, meine my
das Messer knife
die Melone melon
mich me
die Milch milk
das Mineralwasser mineral water
das Minigolf crazy golf
die Minute (pl Minuten) minute
mit with, by; mit dem Bus by bus; mit der Fähre by ferry; mit dem Zug by train
die Mittagspause lunch break
der Mittwoch Wednesday
möchte (mögen) (I) would like (to like)
der Montag Monday; am

Montag on Monday
montags on Mondays
morgen tomorrow
der Morgen morning; Guten Morgen! Good morning!
München Munich
das Museum museum
muss (müssen) (I) have to (to have to); muss ich …? do I have to …?
die Mutter (pl Mütter) mother

N

nach to, towards
die Nachspeise (pl Nachspeisen) dessert
nächste next
die Nacht (pl Nächte) night; gute Nacht goodnight
der Name name
die Nationalität nationality
neben next to, near
nehme (I) take, (I)'ll take
nehmen to take
nein no
neu new
neun nine
neunzehn nineteen
neunzig ninety
nicht not; nicht wahr? isn't it? etc; nicht weit von … not far from …
nichts nothing
die Nieren (pl) kidneys
nimmt (nehmen) (he/she/it) takes (to take)
noch another, more; noch ein(en) … another …; sonst noch etwas? anything else?
der November November
die Nudeln (pl) noodles
null nought, zero

die Nummer number
die Nusstorte nut gateau

O

der Ober waiter
das Obst fruit
oder or
ohne without
der Oktober October
die Orange (pl Orangen) orange
der Orangensaft orange juice
das Österreich Austria
der Österreicher/die Österreicherin Austrian man/woman

P

das Päckchen small pack, packet
die Packung carton
das Parfum perfume
der Parkplatz car park
die Party (pl Partys) party
die Person person
der Platz seat; square
der Polizist/die Polizistin police officer (m/f)
die Pommes frites (pl) chips
die Post post office
die Pralinen (pl) chocolates
der Programmierer/die Programmiererin computer programmer (m/f)
Prost! Cheers!

R

das Rathaus town hall
die Rechnung bill
rechts right, to the right
regnen to rain; es regnet it's raining
der Reis rice

reisen to travel
der Reisescheck (pl Reiseschecks) traveller's cheque
reservieren to reserve, to book
die Reservierung reservation, booking
das Restaurant restaurant
der Rinderbraten roast beef
das Rindfleisch beef
der Rotwein red wine
der Ruhetag rest day
das Rumpsteak rump steak

S

die Sahne cream
der Salat salad
der Samstag Saturday; langer Samstag 'long Saturday'
samstags on Saturdays
der Sauerbraten braised beef marinated in vinegar
der Schinken ham
das Schinkenbrötchen ham roll
schlafen to sleep
schläft (he/she/it) sleeps
schließen to close
der Schlüssel key
schnell quick, quickly
das Schnitzel cutlet
die Schokolade chocolate, drinking chocolate
die Schokoladentorte chocolate gateau
schon already
schön nice, beautiful
der Schotte/die Schottin Scottish man/woman
schreibt (schreiben) (one) writes/spells (to write)
die Schreibwaren (pl) stationery
der Schuh (pl Schuhe) shoe

das Schweinefleisch pork
das Schweinekotelett pork chop
die Schweiz Switzerland
die Schwester sister
das Schwimmbad swimming pool
schwimmen to swim
sechs six
sechzehn sixteen
sechzig sixty
der See lake
die See sea
sehen to see
sein, seine his, its
der Sekretär/die Sekretärin secretary (m/f)
der September September
sicher certainly
Sie you (formal singular and plural)
sie she, they
sieben seven
siebzehn seventeen
siebzig seventy
sieht (sehen) (he/she/it) sees
sind (sein) (we/you/they) are (to be)
der Sohn (pl Söhne) son
soll (sollen) (I) should (to ought to); soll ich …? should I …?
der Sonnabend Saturday
der Sonntag Sunday
sonst noch etwas? anything else?
der Spanier/die Spanierin Spanish man/woman
die Speisekarte menu
die Spezialitäten (pl) specialities
spielen to play
die Sportabteilung sports department

sprechen to speak; sprechen Sie langsamer! speak more slowly!
spricht (he/she/it) speaks
das Stadion stadium
die Stadt (pl Städte) town
die Stadtmitte town centre
das Stadttheater civic theatre
das Stehcafé 'standing café'
stehen to stand
der Steward/die Stewardess steward/stewardess
der Stock floor
die Straße street, road
die Straßenbahn tram
das Stück piece
der Student/die Studentin (f pl Studentinnen) student (m/f)
suche (suchen) (I)'m looking for (to look for)
die Suppe soup
die Süßwarenabteilung confectionery department

T

das T-Shirt T-shirt
der Tag (pl Tage) day; guten Tag good day, good afternoon
die Tagessuppe soup of the day
das Taxi (pl Taxis) taxi
die Tasche bag, handbag
die Tasse (pl Tassen) cup
der Tee tea
das Telefon telephone
die Telefonnummer telephone number
die Terrasse terrace

teuer expensive

die Tochter (pl Töchter) daughter

die Toilette (pl Toiletten) toilet

die Tomate (pl Tomaten) tomato

das Tomatenbrötchen tomato roll

die Tomatensuppe tomato soup

die Torte cake, gateau

der Tourist (pl Touristen) tourist

die Trauben (pl) grapes

trinke (trinken) (I) drink (to drink)

Tschüs! Bye!

der Tunfisch tuna

der Tunfischsalat tuna salad

U

die U-Bahn underground (train)

die Uhr o'clock

um at, round

umsteigen to change (transport)

und and

unser, unsere our

das Untergeschoss basement

die Universität university

V

der Vater father

verheiratet married

der Verkäufer/die Verkäuferin sales assistant, stallholder (m/f), salesman/ saleswoman

das Verkehrsamt tourist information office

das Verkehrsbüro tourist information office

der Verkehrsverein tourist information office

versprechen to promise

verspricht (he/she/it) promises

verstehe (verstehen) (I) understand (to understand)

vielleicht perhaps

vier four

der Viertelliter ¼ litre

vierzehn fourteen

vierzig forty

voll full

vom … bis zum … from the … to the …

von from

der Vorname first name

die Vorspeise (pl Vorspeisen) starter

vorstellen to introduce

W

der Waliser/die Waliserin Welshman/Welshwoman

wann? when?

das Warenhaus department store

warm warm

warten to wait

was? what?; was für …? what kind of …?

das Wasser water

wechseln to change (money)

der Wegweiser store guide

der Wein wine

weiß white

der Weißwein white wine

die Weißwurst Munich white veal sausage

weit far

welche? which?; von welchem Gleis? from which platform?; welche Linie? which number/line?

werden: werden Sie bedient? are you being served?

wie? how?; wie geht es Ihnen?/wie geht's? how are you?; wie lange? how long?

wiederholen to repeat; wiederholen Sie! repeat it!

Wiedersehen 'bye

Wien Vienna

das Wiener Schnitzel breaded veal cutlet

wir we

wo? where?

die Woche week

woher? where from?

wohne (wohnen) (I) live (to live)

die Wurst sausage

Z

zahlen to pay

zehn ten

die Zeitung (pl Zeitungen) newspaper

das Zimmer (pl Zimmer) room

der Zimmernachweis accommodation service

zu to; zu Fuß on foot

der Zug train

zum to the (m/nt); zum Trinken? to drink?

zur to the (f)

der Zuschlag supplement

zwanzig twenty

zwei two

zweimal twice

zweite second; die zweite Straße the second road

im zweiten Stock on the second floor

zweiter Klasse second class (ticket)

die Zwiebeln (pl) onions

zwo two

zwölf twelve

English–German glossary

A

a, an ein/eine
able: to be able to können
accommodation service
der Zimmernachweis
all alles
allowed: to be allowed to
dürfen
already schon
also auch
am bin (from sein to be)
American der Amerikaner
(m)/die Amerikanerin (f)
and und, u. (abbreviated)
another … noch (ein/
eine/einen) …
to answer antworten
anything: anything else?
sonst noch etwas?
apple der Apfel (pl Äpfel)
apple cake der
Apfelkuchen
apple juice der Apfelsaft
April der April
architect der Architekt
are sind (from sein to be)
arrival die Ankunft
to arrive ankommen
(separable)
to ask fragen
at an, bei, um; at ten
o'clock um zehn Uhr
August der August
Australian der Australier
(m)/die Australierin (f)
Austria Österreich (nt)
Austrian der Österreicher
(m)/die Österreicherin (f)

B

bag die Tasche
banana die Banane (pl
Bananen)
bank die Bank

bar die Bar
basement das
Untergeschoss
Basle Basel
bath das Bad
Bavarian (dialect)
Bayerisch
Bavarian (man) der Bayer
to be sein
beautiful schön
beef das Rindfleisch
beef: braised beef
marinated in vinegar der
Sauerbraten
beer das Bier
behind hinter
big groß
bill die Rechnung
bingo das Lotto
biscuits die Kekse (pl)
Bolzano (town in
Northern Italy) Bozen
book das Buch (pl Bücher)
to book reservieren
booking die Reservierung
bottle die Flasche
boy der Junge (pl Jungen)
bread roll das Brötchen
(pl Brötchen)
breakfast das Frühstück
bus der Bus; by bus mit
dem Bus
bus stop die
Bushaltestelle
but aber
to buy kaufen
by (transport) mit
Bye! Tschüs!,
Wiedersehen!

C

cake die Torte
cake shop die Konditorei
calf's liver die Kalbsleber

called: to be called heißen
campsite der
Campingplatz
can (to be able) kann
(können); can I help you?
bitte schön?
can die Dose
Canadian der Kanadier
(m)/die Kanadierin (f)
car das Auto
car park der Parkplatz
carton der Karton, die
Packung
to cash einlösen
(separable)
cash desk die Kasse
cathedral der Dom
cent der Cent (pl Cent)
certainly sicher
to change (money)
wechseln
to change (transport)
umsteigen (separable)
checkpoint der
Kontrollpunkt
Cheers! Prost!
cheese der Käse
cheesecake der
Käsekuchen
chemist's Apotheke
cherry die Kirsche (pl
Kirschen)
cherry brandy das
Kirschwasser
chicken das Hähnchen
child das Kind (pl Kinder)
children's playground der
Kinderspielplatz
chips die Pommes frites
(pl)
chocolate die Schokolade;
chocolates die Pralinen
(pl)

chocolate gateau die Schokoladentorte

civic theatre das Stadttheater

to close schließen

closed geschlossen

club der Club (pl Clubs)

coffee der Kaffee (pl Kaffee)

coke, cola die Cola

cold meats der Aufschnitt

colleague der Kollege (m)/die Kollegin (f)

Cologne Köln

to come kommen; that comes to … das macht …

computer Computer (pl Computer)

computer programmer der Programmierer (m)/ die Programmiererin (f)

confectionery department die Süßwarenabteilung

corner die Ecke

to cost kosten

country das Land

crazy golf das Minigolf

cream die Sahne

credit card die Kreditkarte

cup die Tasse (pl Tassen)

customer der Kunde (m); die Kundin (f)

cutlet das Schnitzel

D

daughter die Tochter (pl Töchter)

day der Tag (pl Tage)

December der Dezember

department die Abteilung

department store das Kaufhaus, das Warenhaus

departure die Abfahrt

dessert die Nachspeise

(pl Nachspeisen)

dish das Gericht (pl Gerichte)

to do machen

double room das Doppelzimmer

to drink trinken

drinking chocolate die Schokolade

Dutchman der Holländer

E

easily leicht

to eat essen

eight acht

eighteen achtzehn

eighty achtzig

eleven elf

England England (nt)

Englishman der Engländer

Englishwoman die Engländerin

enjoy your meal! guten Appetit!

euro der Euro (pl Euro)

evening der Abend; good evening guten Abend

everything alles

excuse me entschuldigen Sie

expensive teuer

F

far weit; not far from … nicht weit von …

father der Vater

February der Februar

ferry die Fähre; by ferry mit der Fähre

fifteen fünfzehn

fifty fünfzig

to find finden

first erst; first class (ticket) erster Klasse; on the first floor im ersten Stock; the first road die

erste Straße; first name der Vorname

fish der Fisch

five fünf

floor der Stock; on the first floor im ersten Stock

food hall die Lebensmittelabteilung

foot der Fuß; on foot zu Fuß

for für, bei (working)

foreigner der Ausländer (m)/die Ausländerin (f)

fork die Gabel

forty vierzig

fountain der Brunnen

four vier

fourteen vierzehn

France Frankreich (nt)

free frei

fresh frisch; fresh fruit frisches Obst

Friday der Freitag

friend der Freund (pl Freunde)

from aus, von; from the … to the … vom … bis zum …

fruit das Obst

full voll

G

garlic der Knoblauch

German deutsch (adjective); in German auf Deutsch; German man/ woman der/die Deutsche

Germany Deutschland (nt)

get off (transport) aussteigen (separable)

get on (transport) einsteigen (separable)

gift das Geschenk (pl Geschenke)

girl das Mädchen

to give geben
glass das Glas
to go gehen
good gut; good afternoon, good day guten Tag; good evening guten Abend; good morning guten Morgen
good (of food): it was good es hat gut geschmeckt
goodbye auf Wiedersehen
goodnight gute Nacht
gram das Gramm
grapes die Trauben (pl)
ground floor das Erdgeschoss

H

half halb; half a kilo ein halbes Kilo
ham der Schinken
ham roll das Schinkenbrötchen
handbag die Tasche
has hat (from haben to have)
to have haben
to have to müssen
he er
Hello! Guten Tag!
to help helfen
her ihr/ihre
here hier
here you are bitte schön
herring salad der Heringssalat
his sein/seine
hobby das Hobby (pl Hobbys)
to hold halten
hotel das Hotel
house das Haus (pl Häuser)

household goods department die Haushaltswarenabteilung
housewife die Hausfrau
how? wie?; how are you? wie geht es Ihnen?/wie geht's?; how long? wie lange?
hundred hundert
husband der Mann

I

I ich
ice cream das Eis; mixed ice cream gemischtes Eis
in, into in; in the (m/nt) im
information die Auskunft
international international
to introduce vorstellen (separable)
Ireland Irland (nt)
Irishman der Ire
Irishwoman die Irin
is ist (from sein to be)
isn't it? etc nicht wahr?
it er/sie/es
Italian der Italiener (m)/die Italienerin (f)
its sein/seine/ihr/ihre

J

January der Januar
journalist (f) die Journalistin
July der Juli
June der Juni

K

key der Schlüssel
kidneys die Nieren (pl)
kilo(gram) das Kilo
knife das Messer
to know (to be acquainted with) kennen

knuckle of pork das Eisbein

L

lake der See
to learn lernen
leather bag die Ledertasche (pl Ledertaschen)
leather goods department die Lederwarenabteilung
leave abfahren (separable)
left, to the left links
lemonade die Limonade
to like mögen; I would like ich möchte
likewise ebenfalls
line (transport) die Linie
litre der Liter
to live wohnen
liver die Leber; calf's liver die Kalbsleber
local lokal
to look for suchen
love: I'd love to gern
lunch break die Mittagspause

M

main course das Hauptgericht (pl Hauptgerichte)
main station der Hauptbahnhof
to make machen
man der Mann
March der März
marital status der Familienstand
market square der Marktplatz
married verheiratet
May der Mai
may I ...? darf ich ...? (from dürfen to be allowed to)

me mich
meal: enjoy your meal! guten Appetit!
mechanic der Mechaniker (m)/die Mechanikerin (f)
melon die Melone
men's fashions die Männermode
mention: don't mention it bitte
menu die Speisekarte
milk die Milch
mineral water das Mineralwasser
minute die Minute (pl Minuten)
mixed gemischt; mixed ice cream gemischtes Eis
Monday der Montag; on Monday am Montag; on Mondays montags
money das Geld
more noch
morning der Morgen
mother die Mutter (pl Mütter)
Mr der Herr
Mrs die Frau
Munich München
museum das Museum
my mein/meine

N

name der Name
nationality die Nationalität
near neben
nearby in der Nähe
new neu
newspaper die Zeitung (pl Zeitungen)
next nächste
next to neben
nice schön
night die Nacht (pl Nächte)

nine neun
nineteen neunzehn
ninety neunzig
no nein; kein/keine
noodles die Nudeln (pl)
not nicht
not a, not any kein/keine
nothing nichts
nought null
November der November
number die Nummer
number (transport) die Linie
nut gateau die Nusstorte

O

occupation der Beruf
occupied besetzt
o'clock Uhr; four o'clock vier Uhr
October der Oktober
office das Büro
old alt
old (part of) town die Altstadt
once einmal
one eins; ein/eine; man
onions die Zwiebeln (pl)
open geöffnet
opposite gegenüber
or oder
orange die Orange (pl Orangen)
orange juice der Orangensaft
ought to soll (sollen)
our unser/unsere
out of aus
over there dort drüben

P

pack, packet das Päckchen, die Packung
parents die Eltern (pl)
party die Party (pl Partys)
pay zahlen, bezahlen

perfume das Parfum
perhaps vielleicht
person die Person
piece das Stück
pineapple die Ananas
platform das Gleis; from which platform? von welchem Gleis?
to play spielen
please bitte
pleased to meet you (es) freut mich
police officer der Polizist (m)/die Polizistin (f)
pork das Schweinefleisch
pork chop das Schweinekotelett
pork cutlet with peppers and mushrooms das Jägerschnitzel
post office die Post
pot das Kännchen
prawn cocktail der Krabbencocktail
present das Geschenk (pl Geschenke)
to promise versprechen
pub das Gasthaus

Q

quarter of a litre der Viertelliter
quick, quickly schnell

R

railway station der Bahnhof
to rain regnen; it's raining es regnet
to read lesen
to recommend empfehlen
red wine der Rotwein
to repeat wiederholen; repeat it! wiederholen Sie!
reservation die Reservierung

to reserve reservieren
restaurant das Restaurant
return (ticket) hin und zurück
rice der Reis
right, to the right rechts
river der Fluss
road die Straße
roast beef der Rinderbraten
roll das Brötchen (pl Brötchen)
room das Zimmer (pl Zimmer)
round um
rump steak das Rumpsteak
to run laufen

S
salad der Salat
sales assistant der Verkäufer (m)/die Verkäuferin (f)
Saturday der Samstag, der Sonnabend; on Saturdays samstags
sausage die Wurst
Scotsman, Scottish man der Schotte
Scotswoman, Scottish woman die Schottin
sea die See
seat der Platz
second zweite; the second road die zweite Straße; on the second floor im zweiten Stock; second class (ticket) zweiter Klasse
secretary der Sekretär (m)/die Sekretärin (f)
to see sehen
September der September

served: are you being served? werden Sie bedient?
seven sieben
seventeen siebzehn
seventy siebzig
she sie
shoe der Schuh (pl Schuhe)
shopping centre das Einkaufszentrum
should soll (sollen); should I …? soll ich …?
shower die Dusche
single (ticket) einfach
single room das Einzelzimmer
sister die Schwester
six sechs
sixteen sechzehn
sixty sechzig
to sleep schlafen
slow, slowly langsam; more slowly langsamer
small klein
something etwas
son der Sohn (pl Söhne)
sorry: I'm sorry es tut mir leid
soup die Suppe; soup of the day die Tagessuppe
Spanish man der Spanier
Spanish woman die Spanierin
to speak sprechen; speak more slowly! sprechen Sie langsamer!
specialities die Spezialitäten (pl)
to spell schreiben
spoon der Löffel
sports department die Sportabteilung
square der Platz
stadium das Stadion

stallholder der Verkäufer (m)/die Verkäuferin (f)
to stand stehen
standing café das Stehcafé
starter die Vorspeise (pl Vorspeisen)
state: German state das Land
station der Bahnhof
stationery die Schreibwaren (pl)
steamer der Dampfer
steward der Steward
stewardess die Stewardess
to stop halten
store guide der Wegweiser
straight on geradeaus
strange fremd
street die Straße
student der Student (m)/die Studentin (f)
Sunday der Sonntag
supplement der Zuschlag
surname der Familienname
to swim schwimmen
swimming pool das Schwimmbad
Switzerland die Schweiz

T
to take nehmen
taxi das Taxi (pl Taxis)
tea der Tee
teacher der Lehrer (m)/die Lehrerin (f)
to telephone anrufen (separable)
telephone das Telefon
telephone number die Telefonnummer
ten zehn
terrace die Terrasse

thank you (very much)
danke (schön)
that (opposite of this)
das; that is das ist; that
comes to ... das macht ...
that (conjunction) dass
the der (m), die (f or pl),
das (nt)
their ihr/ihre
then dann
there da, dort
there is/are es gibt
these diese; these are
das sind
they sie
third dritte; on the third
floor im dritten Stock
thirteen dreizehn
thirty dreißig
this dieser/diese/dieses
three drei
three times dreimal
Thursday der Donnerstag
ticket die Fahrkarte
till (cash till) die Kasse
tin die Dose
to zu, nach; to the (m/nt)
zum; to the (f) zur
today heute
toilet die Toilette (pl
Toiletten)
tomato die Tomate (pl
Tomaten)
tomato roll das
Tomatenbrötchen
tomato soup die
Tomatensuppe
tomorrow morgen
too auch
tourist der Tourist (pl
Touristen)
tourist information
office das Verkehrsamt,
das Verkehrsbüro, der
Verkehrsverein
towards nach

town die Stadt (pl
Städte)
town centre die
Stadtmitte
town hall das Rathaus
train der Zug; by train mit
dem Zug
tram die Straßenbahn;
by tram mit der
Straßenbahn
to travel fahren, reisen
traveller's cheque
der Reisescheck (pl
Reiseschecks)
T-shirt das T-Shirt
Tuesday der Dienstag
tuna der Tunfisch; tuna
salad der Tunfischsalat
twelve zwölf
twenty zwanzig
twice zweimal
two zwei, zwo

U

underground (train) die
U-Bahn
to understand verstehen
unemployed arbeitslos
university die Universität
until bis (zum)

V

vacant frei
veal das Kalbfleisch
veal: breaded veal cutlet
das Wiener Schnitzel
Vienna Wien
to visit besuchen
visitor der Besucher (m)

W

to wait warten
waiter der Ober
waitress die Kellnerin
walking, on foot zu Fuß
warm warm

water das Wasser
we wir
Wednesday der Mittwoch
week die Woche
well gut
Welshman der Waliser
Welshwoman die
Waliserin
what? was?; what kind of
...? was für ...?
when? wann?
where? wo?; where from?
woher?
which? welche?; which
number (transport)?
welche Linie?; (from)
which platform?
welchem Gleis?
white weiß
white (veal) sausage die
Weißwurst
white wine der Weißwein
wife die Frau
willingly gern
wine der Wein
with mit
without ohne
woman die Frau
women's fashions die
Frauenmode
to work arbeiten
to write schreiben

Y

year das Jahr (pl Jahre);
... years old Jahre ... alt
yes ja
you du, ihr, Sie, man; to
you (formal singular and
plural) Ihnen
your dein/deine, euer/
eure, Ihr/Ihre

Z

zero null